C000110251

Everyday Heroes

A Celebration of Volunteering in Ireland

Fiona Murdoch

With a Foreword by Marian Finucane

VERITAS

First published 2004 by
Veritas Publications
7/8 Lower Abbey Street
Dublin 1
Ireland
Email publications@veritas.ie
Website www.veritas.ie

ISBN 1 85390 830 4

Copyright © Fiona Murdoch, 2004

The material in this publication is protected by copyright law. Except as may be permitted by law, no part of the material may be reproduced (including by storage in a retrieval system) or transmitted in any form or by any means, adapted, rented or lent without the written permission of the copyright owners. Applications for permissions should be addressed to the publisher.

A catalogue record for this book
is available from the British Library.

Photo of Adi Roche © Julien Behal;
photo of Des Bishop © Linda Brownlee

Designed by Colette Dower
Printed in the Republic of Ireland by Betaprint, Dublin

Veritas books are printed on paper made from the wood pulp of managed forests. For every tree felled, at least one tree is planted, thereby renewing natural resources.

Contents

Foreword

The stories in this book make primarily for a good read, providing insight into what moves people to engage or volunteer in the first place, as well as giving information on an extraordinarily wide range of volunteer activities.

At a time when there is much criticism of the more 'well off' Irish society – cash rich and time poor – these stories may serve as an inspiration to many to find the time for volunteer work. For what is very clear is that *Everyday Heroes* is not about self-congratulatory 'do goodery', but rather about people who have gained enormous personal satisfaction and enrichment themselves through their voluntary work.

Ireland could still not operate as a proper society without the armies of volunteers who give of their time in areas like Hospice, St Vincent De Paul, Simon, Tidy Towns, the GAA, the Third World charities; the list is endless.

Sometimes, the volunteers may feel under-appreciated, but this connection between the person and the state in the delivering of important services is one of the most valuable and healthy phenomenona in our society. It makes for a happy win/win situation where the volunteers' reward is as great as those who receive the services.

Marian Finucane

Acknowledgements

Firstly, I wish to thank all those who courageously agreed to be interviewed for this book; without them, *Everyday Heroes* would never have come into being. Without exception, I was touched by their honesty, their commitment and their tremendous desire to make this world a better place. I thank them sincerely for sharing their stories and their vision, which I have no doubt will enlighten and inform, challenge and inspire.

My grateful thanks go, also, to Veritas director, Maura Hyland, for asking me to write the book in the first place and to my editorial team, Helen Carr and Majella Cullinane, for their support and assistance. My special thanks go to Marian Finucane for taking time out of her busy schedule to write the foreword. Marian herself has undertaken extensive voluntary work, primarily for the hospice movement – not only in Ireland, but also overseas; she recently opened The Lizo Nobanda Hospice in South Africa, which offers care and dignity to dying children and their families.

Everyday Heroes has been made possible by the support, encouragement and advice of a diverse range of people – family, friends, acquaintances and 'contacts' – too numerous to mention. To everyone who has contributed to this book – not least those interviewees whose stories, due to constraints of space, unfortunately did not make it to the final draft – I am extremely grateful.

Introduction

'W'hat's the title?' people always eagerly enquire when they hear you're writing a book, especially when you've asked them if you can include their story in the publication. It was precisely this question I dreaded being asked whenever I approached a volunteer for inclusion in this book. All along the working title was *Everyday Heroes* and I was pretty sure that most, if not all, of the people I hoped to interview would balk at the idea of appearing in a book with such a name; 'hero' not being a word they would easily apply to themselves. I'm not a very accomplished liar, so I was mightily relieved that only one or two people posed the question. The few who did were greeted with a mumbled reply of, 'Well, it's up to the publishers really' before I swiftly changed the subject or started firing questions, leaving them with little opportunity to pursue the subject further!

I do indeed feel that the people who appear in this book are heroic, but I decided to add the description 'everyday', knowing that there are tens of thousands of other people in Ireland today who are also devoting phenomenal amounts of time, energy and resources to worthy causes. In fact, Irish people are exemplary in carrying out voluntary work with a third of us engaged in some kind of volunteering. According to Oxfam Ireland, we are twice as likely as people in most other European countries to volunteer. It was with the idea of celebrating this spirit of activism in Ireland that Veritas approached me; they were keen to publish a collection of volunteering stories. A few people who appear in this book are well known, either for their high-profile volunteering or because their day-to-day work is carried out in the public arena, but most are private citizens going about their good works quietly and away from the spotlight. Whether famous or unsung, they do share one thing in common, however – they inspire, provoke and make a difference.

A broadly accepted definition of volunteering is 'the commitment of time and energy for the benefit of society, local communities, individuals outside the immediate family, the environment or other causes.' This can be in an organisation setting or it can be quite informal, such as spending time with an elderly person who lives alone or taking the neighbours' children off their hands once in a while. According to studies carried out by the National College of Ireland in recent years, the total amount of time given to voluntary work per year is equivalent to some 96,454 full-time workers.

Ireland's remarkable spirit of volunteering was witnessed throughout the country in June 2003 in a way that it had almost certainly never been seen before. Thirty thousand volunteers were needed to ensure the smooth running of the 2003 Special Olympics World Summer Games – twenty thousand during the Games themselves and another ten thousand in the host towns the week beforehand. Incredibly, more than the requisite number volunteered and five thousand willing helpers ended up on a waiting list! Chief Executive Officer Mary Davis never worried that she would get all the help she needed. 'We were always confident we would get enough volunteers,' she says. 'The thing that was difficult for us was to get across to them, during their training sessions, the perception of what it would be like for them. That it would be like nothing they had ever done before –

an experience they would treasure, remember, carry away forever in their lives. People made huge personal sacrifices to make the Games happen; they gave selflessly and put in so much effort; that's what made the Games successful. I've no doubt it was a great, great experience for all the volunteers and I'm sure they found that they got an awful lot more out of it than they ever thought they would.'

People volunteer for a wide variety of reasons, including the satisfaction of seeing results, the feel-good factor, to meet new people, to raise money for a cause, to get a better balance in life, or simply because they're asked. Often people do not even recognise what they do as volunteering, such as giving blood, helping in their local church or getting involved in school activities. A number of people who appear in this book have been motivated by personal tragedy: their own suffering has prompted them to reach out to others. Quite a few mentioned their religious beliefs as a contributory factor to their volunteering. Several young people, while feeling somewhat disillusioned with organised religion, alluded to their belief that Jesus Christ had been very much a hands-on socially active man, as well as a preacher.

Everyone agreed that they benefited enormously from their volunteering, many saying that they received far more from the experience than they ever gave. They talked about how their voluntary work had enriched their lives and, in many cases, had helped them find personal happiness. Most of those who had volunteered in developing countries talked about how much they had enjoyed experiencing a different culture and meeting a variety of people. Several of them also spoke about the culture shock of returning to Ireland and recognising just how materialistic and consumerist we are and how spoiled Irish children are in comparison to those living in poor countries.

Everybody likes a good story and *Everyday Heroes* is simply a collection of different people's stories. But not any old stories! In compiling the book it was important for me to dig out particularly interesting tales that would grip the reader as well as inform and, hopefully, inspire. Many of the people who appear in the book are exceptional in one way or another; and their stories deserve to be heard. Most interviews were carried out face-to-face and took place in a variety of venues – some in people's homes, others in workplaces or where people volunteered, others in cafés or bars. Amnesty International's Freedom Café on Fleet Street became a regular haunt over my months of interviewing.

It quickly became apparent to me, during the course of my research, that volunteering cuts across all kinds of boundaries – age, class, religion, the lot. The youngest volunteer I interviewed was six, the oldest was in her seventies. I purposely decided to include a chapter about foreign nationals who contribute to their local communities in Ireland. It seems to me that immigrants – whether asylum seekers, refugees or economic migrants – get far too much bad press and I wanted to do a little to redress the balance. It took no time at all to find non-nationals who are making a significant contribution to their local communities, not just for the benefit of other foreign nationals, but also for the enrichment of the lives of Irish people. I, for one, am delighted that this country has become a more diverse and colourful nation in recent years. It certainly makes life a lot more interesting!

It was a delight and a privilege to interview each and every person who appears in this book and meeting them has left me without any doubt that the spirit of volunteering is alive and well in Ireland today. I no longer feel the need I did a year ago to bemoan the fact that Irish society has become apparently so greedy and self-serving. There is plenty of reason to look around and celebrate the fact that people are indeed concerned for the well-being of others, beyond their own circle of family and friends. And the really good news, judging from the school pupils and other young people I came across, is that the spirit of volunteering is equally alive and well among the younger generation. I used to think that voluntary work was primarily for retired people or homemakers whose children had flown the nest, but that notion has been well and truly dispelled! A good number of the interviewees lead very busy lives and, as it happened, several are separated women who make time to volunteer on top of their single-parenting and work commitments.

A few of the interviewees talked about absorbing a volunteering spirit from their own parents' activism which, as a mother, I found particularly challenging. None of the parenting manuals I've ever read has even touched on this subject! But it does make sense: that a child brought up in a home where there is an interest in the welfare of others outside the family is far more likely to develop into the kind of young person whose interests extend beyond career, money, nice house and so on. My own parents have been on a myriad of committees (social, educational and religious) for as long as I can remember and, from an early age, I was aware that my grandfather, Victor Bewley, was extraordinarily devoted to the cause of Irish Travellers. So much so that in 1974 he was appointed national adviser to the government on the programme of the settlement of Travellers, an unsalaried post he was to hold for fourteen years. Following his death in 1999, he was described by *The Irish Times* as 'one of the state's most notable philanthropists'.

Researching this book and giving the matter some thought has led me to conclude that everybody has an obligation to help those less fortunate than themselves: you don't have to be in a position of status or in the public eye to help another person. I am not engaged in any outstanding voluntary work myself – I am involved, to an extent, in church activities and I get involved in the odd bit of fundraising, but I do not do anything extraordinary, the way many of the people in this book do. Meeting them has certainly made me question how I spend my time and use my resources and I am quite sure that readers of this book will be challenged in the same kind of way that I have been. It's been interesting, too, to look back and reflect on what my upbringing would have been like without the unpaid input, say, of Sunday School teachers, youth leaders, sports coaches and Brownie/Girl Guide leaders.

It's all too easy to say, 'I've nothing to offer', but the truth is that everybody has some kind of ability or skill that they can use for the good of the wider community. And, while there is a huge amount of good work going on, there is so much more that needs to be done. The appendix at the back of the book lists just a few of the many organisations that are dependent on the lifeblood of voluntary help, as well as donations. For those who are interested in pursuing some kind of volunteering, but who are unsure where exactly to offer their time and skills, Volunteering Ireland provides the ideal first port of call. It acts as a link between a wide range of organisations and individuals who wish to undertake meaningful voluntary work.

To quote from John F. Kennedy, former President of the United States: 'Ask not what your country can do for you, but what can you do for your country.' Perhaps each of us should ask ourselves that question – not just from a national point of view, but also, by extending our vision beyond our own small island, 'What can we do for the benefit of society at large?' After all, each of us has something to contribute to making this world a better place to live – in our own unique way.

Fiona Murdoch
September 2004

Adi Roche and Duncan Stewart

who go to extraordinary lengths to help people affected by the Chernobyl nuclear disaster

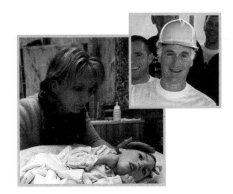

Adi Roche is one of Ireland's most remarkable volunteers. Since walking out of her Aer Lingus job twenty-two years ago, she has devoted phenomenal amounts of time and energy to various causes. Firstly, to the Campaign for Nuclear Disarmament and then to the Chernobyl Children's Project, which she founded in response to the nuclear disaster that occurred in the Ukraine on 26 April 1986. Her devotion to this cause has meant that she has not only become a household name in her native country, but she has also gained recognition in many other parts of the world; and deservedly so.

The Chernobyl Children's Project (CCP) has been responsible for numerous aid convoys to Belarus, the Ukraine and western Russia and for various building projects to help people who, eighteen years later, are still suffering from the appalling consequences of the radiation fallout. More than eleven thousand children have spent time with Irish families (a month away from contamination can add two years to a child's life) and volunteer surgeons, both in Ireland and abroad, have operated on hundreds of sick children. Dozens more have been adopted by Irish families, thanks to the adoption agreement brokered by Adi and CCP patron, Ali Hewson, in 1995. The organisation has grown to such an extent that it now boasts an incredible seven thousand volunteers. There are also ten members of paid staff (six in Ireland, four in Belarus), but incredibly Adi, as executive director, still refuses to draw a salary (and, no, she's not married to a millionaire; her husband, Sean Dunne, is a teacher). In fact, so devoted is Adi to her Chernobyl work that every year she makes the same New Year's Resolution – that she will take a holiday in the coming year. Invariably, this either does not come about or her time away is foreshortened.

The remarkable work undertaken by Adi and CCP has not escaped the notice of high-profile organisations like the UN, UNESCO, UNICEF and the World Health Organisation (WHO). Adi felt extremely honoured when she was invited to give the keynote speech at the UN General Assembly on 26 April 2004, the eighteenth anniversary of the Chernobyl disaster. She also had the opportunity to show delegates the Oscar-winning documentary, *Chernobyl Heart*, which CCP had been involved in making. Produced and directed by independent US film-maker Maryann De Leo, it was shot over a two-year period in Belarus, the country most seriously contaminated by the Chernobyl accident.

In the past three years CCP has been making forays into America in search of funds and volunteers. In fact, all but one of a team of fifty-five surgeons who went out to Belarus in June 2004 were from the US. 'We work with sister organisations in England, Italy, Israel, Canada and Australia and now we're moving into America,' says Adi. 'It is one of the wealthiest nations in the world and so it's there we can get the greatest support. Americans don't know very much about the effects of Chernobyl; in fact, we've discovered that it is the Irish who are top of the class – we are so well-informed in comparison to everyone else. That has been recognised by the UN and I'm so proud to say it. There are non-governmental organisations (NGOs) all over the world working on Chernobyl and yet the UN has chosen CCP as the world's most effective, efficient and largest organisation and they have put us on a scientific body representing all the Chernobyl NGOs in the world. We were kind of gobsmacked when we heard this because it's a very specialised body with many top experts. These guys have all the science and all the knowledge, but now they need to connect with the human reality – the human face, the heart and the soul of the consequences of the tragedy. That's what they'll get from us, and so what we're bringing to it is vital.'

Adi is a dynamo who exudes vast amounts of enthusiasm and optimism. Before the screening of the *Chernobyl Heart* documentary on US television in September 2004 she was extremely hopeful of the results it would bring for CCP. 'You have to believe,' she says. 'You have to say, "We mightn't get a brass farthing out of this, but we might get a hundred thousand. We might even get a million! Who knows?" I'm going to be holding my breath as people watch the documentary and I'm going to watch those phone lines jump out of their sockets because I really believe it's going to happen. I'm planning already; I'm spending in advance because I trust in it so much. If I'd known all those years ago that my job was going to involve having to raise one and a half million every year I would have run screaming to the furthest corner of the planet! What I have to do is trust in the man or woman above, trust in the process and trust in the spirit – the common shared humanity of people and their willingness to transform their passion for life into compassion for their fellow human beings. I see it each and every day. Seven thousand volunteers! It takes all shapes and sizes, creeds and colours.'

Rather than accept any plaudits herself, Adi prefers to deflect any attention she may receive to the countless CCP volunteers. 'This is not about a singular person called Adi Roche,' she says. 'I may be the face of it, but that's it, draw the line there. It's the power of the people behind me. So many amazing, spontaneous things happen in this organisation, I just don't know what the next call is going to be. It might be someone saying, "I can give you five trucks for a convoy," or "I'll sponsor an ambulance for you," or "I'd like to take ten kids" or "I'm a doctor and I'd like to volunteer." Not a day goes by when I don't get a call like that. I would say that the strength of CCP lies in our diversity and in our strong regionalisation. The fact that we have groups the length and breadth of the country means we have this lovely informal root for recruiting volunteers – doctors, nurses, carpenters, plumbers, electricians, teachers, pilots and surgeons. On Easter Sunday this year we sent out €3m worth of aid on the backs of sixteen articulated trucks and sixteen fully equipped ambulances. All donated by the people of Ireland! It's just extraordinary. It's the people of Ireland who have kept this issue alive for the past eighteen years and when I receive awards, like Irish Person of the Year, I always accept them in the name of all the volunteers – the people whose faces and names you will never know. I'm just their mouthpiece. I think it will be written on my tombstone, "She got it for free" because unless I can get something for nothing, then I don't get it. The only reason CCP has got such good media coverage is because of my brass neck, sense of humour and that fire in the belly. The old fire in the belly is, to me, very important.'

CCP now has aid convoys going out to Belarus twice a year and medical teams going out every month. 'Every time they go they save lives,' says Adi. 'And what a privilege to be able to do that for another human being. I just couldn't imagine not being involved in this powerful work; and it is bloody powerful work. I just feel – and I know I'm speaking for all the volunteers when I say this – our lives would be far emptier without this. They'd have far less meaning. As far as I'm concerned, this is what life and living is all about, this is why we're on the planet: we're not just here to chill out, have a good time and feather our own nests. We are here to be shoulder to shoulder, arm in arm, supporting one another – to be just and peaceful to one another and to show huge love to one another. Not to tear each other apart, make war on one another and to suck the earth dry of its resources while expecting it to replenish itself.

'Volunteering is something that is so central to the core of my being and has been for more years than I care to admit. There's such a tremendous power of volunteerism in Ireland; I often say that we have inherited both a culture and a mindset of volunteerism. We almost have an extra gene (I say that in a tongue-in-cheek kind of way) because there seems to be this extra dimension to Irish people and I feel that comes from those who have gone before us. You will find Irish people in the four corners of the earth, literally in every trouble spot on the planet – and I think that's a very powerful contribution that we give to the international community. And I think it's no accident that we are outspoken for the rights of others internationally who suffer at the hands of injustice, like poverty and racism, because we have suffered in similar ways. I think our compassion, our activism and our power of volunteerism lies in our past stories. Basically most people living on this island are the direct descendants of those that survived the Great Irish Famine because of the humanity and compassion of people like those of the Quaker religious faith. They extended the hand of friendship and solidarity to us because they had suffered themselves and I suppose when we see suffering either at a local or international level it's kind of like an echo of something that's reverberating through our own psyche. We have been shaped by those who have gone before; we've inherited a deep sense of justice and a commitment to community. For me, it's to do with respect – regardless of sex, race or class – and I think we can be the torch-bearers in the 21st century where there seems to be a great hopelessness and despair at large in the world. There's so much pain, whether it's Iraq or the AIDS crisis in Africa or Chernobyl.'

Adi believes it is important to be aware of what can be achieved through volunteering. 'I always emphasise that kind, generous words will never feed a hungry baby or heal a broken body,' she says. 'It is in the action of the doing that translates our own positive energy into, say, a blanket, a needle or a syringe, and that's what really saves families, communities and the world at large. It is in our own willingness to do that that we perhaps find our own true selves because there's a great sense of being lost in society. Twenty years ago I was involved in the movement against nuclear power, which was pretty dramatic at the time because the government of the day wanted to build not just one nuclear power station, but four nuclear power stations in Ireland. We canvassed and campaigned very effectively until we got the government to reverse its decision. And that showed me how the power of one can become a collective; by people coming together you can make such a massive difference. It's in working together that we can make a more just society and it's in embracing the dynamic changes we meet in every society that we can bring about a better world for everyone.

'I can't emphasise enough what volunteerism does in Ireland and abroad. I mean this country would come to a standstill, were it not for volunteers. That's a fact. Organisations like Simon and St Vincent de Paul depend so much on the efforts of people and even though we have the famous Celtic tiger, who still seems to be stalking the country, but who hasn't touched everybody's life, there is still that real spirit of willingness to reach out. I mean, there but for the grace of God go any of us. Who knows what our circumstances will be, for example, if there is a terrorist attack on Sellafield or if there is another accident there and we were to become the victims of that radiation fallout? I would hope and pray that it would be the Belarussian people, the Ukrainian people and the Russian people – those whom we are currently helping – who would come and help us because it is in the shadow of each other that we all survive. There's a beautiful Irish saying, *"Is ar scáth a chéile a mhaireann na daoine"*, which translates as "It is in the shadow of each other that we survive." None of us lives as separate entities: even though we live on an island we do not live alone on this planet and the sooner we recognise the interdependency the sooner we will work together at keeping it intact. When I give talks in schools I always say, "Guys, what has taken four billion years to be created – this planet and life on it, as we know it – can disappear in a millisecond. There are no emergency exits and no margins for error, either with a weapon of mass destruction or through environmental damage." So whether, as volunteers, we're working for the environmental movement or for justice in society it's all very much part of the same thing.'

Adi's outstanding commitment to volunteering stems back to her childhood in Clonmel, Tipperary. 'My parents were very active and I suppose the spirit of activism I have came from them because they always believed in giving their neighbour a helping hand,' she says. 'In a sense I've always taken activism for granted, even though when I was growing up I didn't know the words "volunteerism" or "activism", but it was very much a part of our lives – as much as we would eat, breathe or sleep. There was a boys' orphanage near us and we used to go and visit every week; and in my adolescence I was involved with the Girl Guides and the Legion of Mary. Meals on Wheels was always a big part of our lives – our dad used to run it and I often went with him to deliver meals. I saw that not everybody had the privilege and warmth in their lives that we were used to. It was very challenging to see poverty within our community because most of the people we mixed with were similar to ourselves – they did ballet and speech and drama, and they went on holidays. Seeing other people's lives showed us there was another kind of shadow world, which was part of our world: it wasn't in darkest Africa or the Middle East; it was actually right within our own community. I learned what a great blessing it is to give, in my own small way, that it is in giving that we receive.'

Adi herself does not have any children to whom she can pass on her indomitable volunteering spirit and she jokes that, if she did, they would have to be given up for adoption. 'To be honest, I couldn't do the level of work that I do if I had children,' she says. 'Having said that, I do feel as if I have thousands and thousands of children – both in Ireland, because of all the kids I work with in schools and who I adore to bits, and in Belarus because of all the thousands and thousands of kids I work with there. The child I am closest to – my all-time most gorgeous, beautiful child – is a little boy called Alexei that Ali Hewson and myself found when he was four months old and he was dying, in a children's home in Belarus, from the effects of radiation. We brought him to Ireland for treatment and he actually survived against the odds, thanks to the miraculous voluntary work of the surgeons in Temple Street. My sister adopted him and he's just had his ninth birthday. He still has a long road to recovery because he has a lot of surgery ahead of him, but he's a very courageous boy. I'm so close to him. My niece in America, Sinéad de Róiste, who is black Irish, was picked as the Philadelphia Rose for this year's Rose of Tralee festival. She came as an intern to CCP as a volunteer last year and we put together a CCP float for the Rose Parade. It was a pretty phenomenal thing for all of us and Alexei was there too; he was dead chuffed.'

Adi cannot sing the praises of Ali Hewson enough, describing her as 'extraordinary'. 'She has supported me for more years than I can think of,' says Adi. 'She is a quiet supporter who has a very deep mind and a great ability to process information and to look at the way forward. You see, I want to do everything all the time every day and I think every idea is a fantastic one; and, of course, that's not the case. Ali has a much more discerning approach and she puts the brakes on me; she hangs back at times when I want to go all guns blazing, two feet forward, immediately jumping in the deep end. She'd say, "Well, I'm not sure if that's exactly what we should be doing right now; let's take a look at that again." And, of course, the second I sit down and think it through logically I see that that wasn't maybe the right approach, that maybe we should do something else. So Ali is a very powerful force and she is that voice of wisdom. When I'm feeling wrecked I go to her for personal refuge and she minds me, dusts me down and gets me back on my feet again. She's done that many times, I can tell you, because burnout does happen, and it happens regularly, although I'm a bit better now at foreseeing it than I was in the past.'

What motivates Adi to get back on her feet and return to her tireless work? 'Just thinking of those tender moments when you see you are making a difference,' she says. 'Whether it's the life that you've helped save – like when you bring children to Ireland for life-saving treatment and you see them arriving, with their lives ebbing away – and then in a very short period of time you see life returning. The gift of that is just extraordinary and it's such a privilege to be a part of that. Or when you see the big eyes opening up with expectation on people's faces when a truck arrives with aid or the look of relief when staff and patients see medical equipment and medicine being brought into a hospital.

There was one time we brought an incubator into a maternity hospital and literally, while we were still removing the cellophane, there was a mother standing waiting with her new-born baby in her arms. She had a look of such relief. We were there for the plugging in of that machine and that baby's life being saved; we knew that if we'd arrived even five or six hours later the baby would have died. That's what does it for me. And then, in the bigger scheme of things, when you see the Irish government reversing its decision on nuclear power or when you see the support it gives to the victims of Chernobyl.'

'This is not altruism – and I really mean that – I'm doing this as much for my own salvation and my own sanity as anything else. It's all about a love for life and a love for the earth itself. When you think that of all the billions of people on this planet there are no two human beings the same – that each one of us is so gifted, so unique and so special, I think that's extraordinary! We have been so loved into life and that deserves being respected. We cannot sustain destruction to the earth and that is a really key message that Duncan Stewart and I have in common, which is far beyond the work we do in highlighting the Chernobyl issue. It is a much more global message than that. It's about saying, "Let's take a rain check here. Let's stop and observe what we are doing to humanity, to different species and literally to the planet itself because we're destroying it at a rate of knots."'

Community-building is at the core of the CCP philosophy and the organisation works with hospitals, schools, orphanages, mental asylums and families; it is also currently building hospice services. 'It's all about partnership-building because we believe that is the key to restoration,' says Adi. 'The local people get involved without being paid; they're as much volunteers as we are because very much at the basis of every project is the idea that it's not the hand out, but the hand up. And so, together with the Department of Foreign Affairs, we are looking at community-building – rebuilding families rather than people being forced to give away their children because they have no hope. We are looking at how we can end those structures of institutions of mental asylums and orphanages, and the way we can do that is by tackling poverty and powerlessness. And so we have this whole concept of building self-reliance and sustainable development.

'We are building a community centre, which is funded by Pfizer Pharmaceuticals and Development Co-operation Ireland. It's the first of its kind and it's going to break that cycle by providing crisis counselling services, an education centre and refuge facilities for families, for the elderly and for children with disabilities. There's going to be a whole range of services provided – literacy courses, computer courses, everything. It's all about skill-building, helping families in crisis and giving refuge to children who are homeless. What we are trying to do as well is break the cycle of nuclear addiction and so we are making the building an example of how you can work with renewables: it's going to run on a new type of heating system, which uses solar energy and wood energy. They get very severe winters there and we want these people to be energy-independent because the gas supply from Russia is often cut off and then these places are left without any heating at -30 degrees.'

Architect, environmentalist and broadcaster Duncan Stewart was delighted when Adi asked him to act as architect for CCP's building projects because he had always been concerned about 'what was going on' in Belarus in the aftermath of the 1986 disaster. 'I was keen to get involved because I felt there were things I should be doing out there,' he says. 'I've been out two times now with a team of builders and work started on the community centre during my second visit, in October 2003. It is a small model that could be expanded later and could be replicated all over the region as a concept. We want the building to have an indigenous supply of energy because we want to get the people away from reliance on nuclear power. There are still up to twenty nuclear reactors across Russia and into Latvia and the Ukraine that are highly dangerous and similar problems could happen again; it's very, very unpredictable what can happen out there.'

Duncan finds it difficult to put into words exactly how he felt on his first visit to the region. 'There were situations so appalling they defy description,' he says. 'You see such suffering and abandonment of children. The mental asylums were by far the worst because of the amount of children with different types of deformities – physical and intellectual – and the extremities of these were horrific. Then you go to orphanages, where they are obviously very poor and under-facilitated, and it's very difficult because they often don't have any heating or lighting. Can you imagine what it's like in winter when the children get frostbite on their fingers and toes? It's sad, you know. You see a situation where you say, "Right, there's an awful lot to do here." The only thing is to know where do you start scratching the surface. It's a huge problem and we're just doing our little bit with CCP, but really the whole world needs to focus on it. There are two and a half million people who are directly affected by the fallout – seventy per cent are in Belarus, fifteen per cent in western Russia and another fifteen per cent in the Ukraine. The problems are much bigger for the Belarussians, though, because they are living under a dictator who just doesn't care.'

As well as giving architectural advice, Duncan has also spent time shooting footage for a TV documentary. He has interviewed many local people – doctors, scientists, teachers and others actively involved in the region – and he has visited orphanages and mental asylums. He hopes the programme will create more awareness in Ireland and across Europe. 'The intention is to show the Irish story and to show what Irish people are doing out there and the interaction between Belarus and Ireland,' he says. 'I want to get the message across to the 450 million people who are now in the EU because I think Irish people are much more aware than people in most European countries because people like Adi are out there doing so much. But I also want to show Irish people that there are things we can do to help, without even having to go out there. I'd like to see more children and families coming to Ireland so that they can have a break from the extreme conditions in which they are living. The problem is that the dose of nuclear radiation that people are getting from their food and water and their environment means it's constantly building up in their bodies; and any relief from that makes a huge change to their health. Coming to Ireland for even a month makes a huge difference to the level of dosage. There is a region of Belarus, which is the size of Britain and Ireland, that's radioactive and they grow crops and they drink the water there. There's an awful lot that needs to be done to motivate the people because they're very, very disillusioned. There are a lot of good people out there, if you give them an opportunity and show them that what is being done can have long-term benefits not just for them, but also for their communities. I'd like to see Irish people supporting the groups out there that are trying to do things, but which maybe lack finance or resources.

'There's a lot of different things we can do to help people develop enterprises, de-institutionalise orphanages and bring the children more into the communities. I think it's very sad because once children are brought up in that kind of institutional environment their chances of integrating later are greatly reduced. There's a lot that can be done to foster a feeling of community involvement and self-help. Very often mothers are abandoned and left on their own with their kids and often at a certain stage the mother will abandon the children, simply because she has no support and she can't cope. There is very little state benefit because the Belarus government has basically turned its back on the problem. It's almost impossible for mothers on their own to survive, especially if there is a disability in the family – and, remember, the percentage of disability is very high because the effects of radiation have gone into the genes. It is already affecting the next generation and it will go on and on. The problems are not going to go away; they're there for a long, long time to come.'

As an architect, Duncan was determined to get close to the Chernobyl reactor to see what kind of condition it was in. 'The problem with Reactor Four is that only three per cent of the uranium exploded, which means that ninety-seven per cent is still there,' says Duncan. 'And it's very, very precarious because the sarcophagus they built over it is disintegrating. It was built in a panic by the Russians, under very difficult conditions, which wasn't an easy thing to do, and when you think of the number of fire fighters who have died since then caused by their exposure to radiation during that work. I spent a day in the compound with Adi and CCP's photographer Julien Behal* as well as our interpreter and driver. We were exposing ourselves to radiation by being there, but it was only for a short period; we had a guigacounter, which basically tells you the radiation levels from the different isotopes, and it was going completely berserk because the levels were so high. Basically, we found ourselves in incredible places where no human being or any other form of life should be, but I was determined to find out for myself the condition of the sarcophagus. I mean, I knew before I went in that it was disintegrating, but I was shocked by the levels of radioactivity. Probably none of us would have gone in there if we'd known because it's one of those experiences you don't want to have in your life. We found that when we followed the railway track down to a corroded bridge over the Dniper River the radioactivity coming from the river was completely off the scale.'

While the group was in the exclusion zone Duncan went off by himself with his TV camera to shoot some footage for his documentary. It was during this time that he had his terrible accident, from which he is still recovering. He received ten broken ribs, a punctured lung and a host of other injuries, which he has no wish to discuss. 'I fell from quite a height – from a tree, it seems. That's what I've been told, but I've no memory of it. The others went out looking for me and when they found me they brought me to hospital, where I was taken for dead; I was unconscious for three days. I was brought to a small little hospital in a town called Bragin, which is on the border of the exclusion zone and I was very lucky that that hospital was there. In fact, I'm very lucky to be alive; I'd definitely be dead if that hospital hadn't been there. There's no doubt about that. My operations were carried out there, but I was taken from there three days later to a bigger hospital in Gomel, a slightly less contaminated area, still contaminated, but not to the same extent. The ambulance I was taken in was very primitive – ancient, you know. It's so sad, really, that these kinds of vehicles are being used as ambulances. I remember a heavy kind of knocking sensation because the road was very rough and there was no suspension in the vehicle and I remember at one stage the stretcher collapsed because it had completely corroded; there was a commotion as the Russian doctors and nurses came around me. It just shows the types of conditions they have to work in. The medical staff were excellent – their commitment and competence was just incredible and I really appreciate them big time. The educational standards in the region are very high, but they don't appreciate their professionals – doctors are paid a pittance and often have to take a second job in order to survive. They don't have cars and most don't even have a bicycle. It's appalling.'

Ten days after his accident Duncan was flown to Ireland where he spent four weeks in St Vincent's Hospital. It was during this time that the story unfolded about how primitive the conditions had been in the hospitals, in terms of equipment (although Duncan had been oblivious to this at the time). This discovery led to a whole new campaign and, although Duncan was not interested in any publicity that focussed on either him or his accident, he was happy to take the opportunity to launch a new CCP campaign, focussing on the need to send out hospital equipment and ambulances. He valiantly left his hospital bed to make an appearance on *The Late Late Show*. 'Pat Kenny came to visit me in hospital and he asked me when I would come on the show,' says Duncan. 'I said that I wouldn't want to talk about my accident, but I would like to come on and talk about the need for medical equipment. And I told him if I could travel from Bragin to Gomel in an ancient ambulance, then surely I could pop down the road to the RTÉ studios!

'On *The Late Late Show* we also launched our campaign for children with what we call "Chernobyl heart", a form of heart disease that occurs as a consequence of the fallout and which is now being genetically transferred to children. I've been in maybe ten or twelve orphanages and I keep coming across these children who are just fading away because of the condition. There are seven thousand children with this particular ailment and every year one thousand more are added to the list, so it's growing all the time. You see these children lying there and the nurses will tell you that they're on the waiting list for an operation, but most don't get operated on and it's only a matter of time before they die. It's a simple operation if it's performed early on and that's why we decided to campaign to raise funds. As a result, surgeons from Ireland, Canada and the US are going out to operate on these children. So I suppose if any good has come out of my accident it's been an increase in awareness and funds.'

Despite Duncan's near-death experience at Chernobyl, he is determined to make a return visit, although his slow recovery has meant he has had to keep postponing this. He is currently preparing to return in October 2004 with Adi and Julien. But why on earth is he willing to risk his life again? 'Because there's a lot to do,' he says. 'If you went out there you'd be hooked too. The first time you go out you go because you're concerned about the situation and once you're out there and you see the way people are suffering you get kind of locked into the place; you can't walk away from it. There's no turning back because it evokes something that causes you to say, "A little bit of my life in the future is going to go into this cause". You know you can do something and you know you have to take the responsibility to do that.

'I have to get back into the compound because last time I didn't get close enough to the reactor itself to see, as an architect would want to see, the damage caused to this big steel and concrete structure. I need to see the extent of the corrosion because a lot of the welding of the steelwork was defective and, as a consequence, the concrete is disintegrating; it's been leaking and if water's getting in then radioactivity must be getting out. It's going to be very dangerous to go there, but I have to get closer to see the evidence.

'We also have to get the community centre up and running. We have to make sure that it proves to be successful, so that the people can replicate the concept into all the towns and villages of the region. It's all about working with the local communities – coming behind the people and giving them guidance and support because they should always have ownership of the projects. There's no value, in my view, of going out there and just doing superficial aid; it's got to be done at a much deeper level. That's the real challenge. It's all about maintaining consistency over time because these are long-term issues and there are no quick fix solutions. We aim to educate, motivate and train people so that they can take over the projects and run them themselves. It's the only way. We've done so little, really; we're just scratching the surface compared to what has to be done. Having said that, I've met Germans, Dutch, Swedes and Italians out there – there's all different projects happening because there's so much that needs to be done – but I would say that CCP is by far the most successful in terms of its commitment and long-term involvement.'

Duncan's dedication to the cause is remarkable but, like Adi, he refuses to take any credit. 'I'm only a minor player,' he says. 'There are people behind the scenes doing all the work and credit should be going to them because they're doing tremendous work all the time. I don't want to be promoted just because I'm in the public eye and I had an accident. I'd rather see the credit going to those who are doing the work and the people of Belarus who are working for the cause. It's a big turn off when I'm given praise; I don't deserve it because I see so many other people behind the scenes doing such good work. I really shouldn't be given any special attention.

'Ali Hewson has been a stalwart of support – she's very committed and dedicated. Bono has been helpful, too, and U2 were very good to give the proceeds of *The Sweetest Thing* to the cause. That was very, very helpful. Then there's the gang in the office in Cork and the thousands of volunteers throughout the country – you can't start naming them all. And then there's Adi herself, who has incredible energy and commitment; I don't know where she gets it. I'm glad now that she didn't get the Presidency; even though she'd have made a great President, I think it would have been very sad to have missed her from this cause because she's totally obsessed with it, she has great energy and she is great at motivating others. She's a fantastic person who is doing incredible work and she's a great diplomat for Ireland out in Europe and the UN. She well deserves the regard that's out there for the extraordinary work she is doing.'

*Sunday Independent *photographer, Julien Behal, is making his fourth trip to Chernobyl and Belarus in October 2004. He is putting together an exhibition of the pictures he has taken on his visits which, if he gets the necessary sponsorship, will tour Ireland in 2005 in an effort to raise awareness and funds for CCP.*

Mags Riordan and Margaret McKinney

*whose volunteering in Malawi
and Northern Ireland
was prompted by the
tragic deaths
of their sons*

Volunteers are motivated by all kinds of reasons and while Margaret McKinney and Mags Riordan are involved in very different kinds of voluntary work they share one thing in common. For both of them, their tremendous efforts to ease the suffering of others stem from the tragic loss of their sons, who were both young adults when they met their deaths – one in a lonely field in rural Monaghan, the other in the depths of Lake Malawi. Margaret comforts others who have been bereaved or traumatised in Northern Ireland's 'Troubles' and Mags brings food, education and medicine to Cape McClear – the village where her son, Billy, was staying when he died.

The McKinney household in the Falls, west Belfast, was filled with happiness and laughter in the 1970s. Money was tight, but they always had enough to get by. Billy drove a van for the Housing Executive and, with the children that bit older, Margaret spent her mornings cleaning in the local school and the evenings working in a local shop, leaving herself time to be with the couple's four children in the afternoons. 'Money was beginning to come in and things were looking up,' says Margaret. 'We were just starting to really get on our feet, get things done to the house, which we could never have afforded to before and take the kids on holidays. All those things we'd been working towards for years.'

The sound of Brian playing his guitar and singing various Inglebert Humberdink songs reverberated through the house. 'Brian was a great singer; he was always singing,' says Margaret. 'He was the funniest wee lad you could ever imagine and everybody was very fond of him. 'Please Release Me' was his favourite song.'

Ironic, really, given the events that began to unfold on 16 June 1978. Brian, who was twenty-two at the time, was running late for work that morning; he was a gardener for the Housing Executive, and his sister, Linda, offered to give him a lift. The last Margaret ever saw of him was when he headed out the door. 'They all used to come in at about five or half-five for their dinner,' she says. 'There was a knock on the door at about that time and it was one of Brian's work mates. He handed me Brian's wages (in those days you got cash in an envelope). I said, "Where's Brian?" He said Brian hadn't come into work that day. Well, that in itself nearly gave me a heart attack because I knew there was no way he would have missed work. But the lad just gave me the wages and left; he seemed to want to get away.

'I couldn't understand it and when Billy came in I told him what had happened and he went and spoke to one of the IRA 'godfathers' who lived a few streets away. The man told Billy he would see if he could find out what had happened and that he would let us know. The next night he came and told us, "Yes, the IRA do have Brian, but don't be worrying about it. It'll be all right; he'll be home soon." Saturday came and there was still no sign of Brian. Then Sunday, Monday, Tuesday and on Wednesday along came the man and said, "He's been put out of the country." That didn't matter to me because so long as he was alive I knew I was going to see him. So I got bits and pieces gathered up in a suitcase and we collected money among ourselves because I was going to fly over to wherever he was. I knew the first thing he'd do when he got off a ferry would be to ring me, for he'd know I'd be worried sick about him. So we waited for a phone call and every time the phone rang we thought it was Brian. This went on for days. All night we would sit up, crying and praying. It just went on and on.'

After endless days of tortuous waiting and wondering, the 'godfather' returned. 'He just walked in and said, "The IRA don't have Brian," and he walked out again,' says Margaret. 'So we knew something terrible had happened; and that's the way we were left. It was as if we'd been left in the deepest pit in hell with no way out. I went insane and God love the rest of my family – what they had to go through – having to watch me crying morning till night. I don't know who looked after them, who made food for them, who cleaned the house, who did anything. Sandra was only thirteen at the time and, to this day even, I don't know who looked after her. The house had been so happy, with everybody always singing and Brian playing the guitar; it went from that to the deepest pit in hell. I just can't describe the horror; the doctor put me on tranquillisers and I ate them like sweets. After a couple of weeks we knew Brian was dead because we knew rightly there was no way they'd have kept him alive. His older brother Martin, God love him, used to get up very early in the mornings, before anyone else was up and go up to the fields, looking for his body. I'd nobody to talk to and I'd go up to the chapel, kneel at the altar and scream at God. It was complete insanity, but I felt we just needed to have his body.

'The sickness started then – one heart attack after another. We'd been well before that, but after Brian disappeared Billy and I both had heart attacks from the stress. Our health broke down completely and we had to give up work and everything. The neighbours weren't talking to us because the 'godfathers' had put it out that Brian was in France or Mexico and that we were in contact with him. Our Brian in France or Mexico? The longest he had ever been away was a week in Butlin's; and he'd had to come home early because it was breaking his heart to be away.

'I was too scared to talk to anyone – I was too afraid to say or do anything in case I'd anger the IRA and they'd do the same to someone else in my family. I felt terribly intimidated because we live in a highly republican area and in those days if you weren't for them you were against them. I feared being burned out of the house and I used to lie with my face buried in the pillow, sobbing in case anybody would hear me, waiting for the letter box to open and someone to pour petrol in. I spent the whole time wondering how we were going to escape downstairs, if there was a fire. And yet I didn't do anybody any harm in my entire life! I'd never had any interest in organisations or religion or anything; my whole life had been spent trying to rear my children. Anybody who did come to see us would just sit there because it was the horrors even for them, you know. They couldn't understand either why Brian had been taken.'

Brian was 'a wee lad' – standing, as he did, at five feet – and he had been a sickly child, in and out of hospital with chronic asthma. When he was fourteen he had been diagnosed as having the mind of a six-year-old child. He left school soon after that and got a job with the Housing Executive. 'I was so glad he was working on the estate here, planting trees and bushes and doing the grass, because there were so many sectarian murders happening at that time that I was happy to know he was nearby,' says Margaret. 'I didn't know why they had taken him because he didn't do anything to be taken away and never seen again. There was one night the previous week that he didn't come in all night and we were out of our minds because that was unheard of. We were up all night and the next night; it was only after forty-eight hours that he came home. He was in an awful state. I asked him what had happened and he proceeded to tell me that he'd taken part in a robbery. I asked him how much he had got out of it – it was about forty or fifty pounds, which was a fortune then. He didn't need the money, but he probably took part because it made him look like one of the big boys. Billy and I took him to the clubhouse they had raided and made him apologise and give back his share of the money. It was a week later that the IRA took Brian and they took one of the other lads who was involved in the robbery too. The other young ones got away across the border and to different places. I often wonder what kind of person could take away our child like that.'

To this day, Margaret still does not have the answer to that question. It took years before the doom and gloom in the McKinney household began to lift. The first ray of hope came four years later when Sandra had a baby, Laura. 'I can truthfully say that the baby was the first thing that brought joy, life and hope into our home,' says Margaret. 'Laura gave us a reason to live; we reared her here and she was a wonderful, wonderful child. I always felt that God sent her specially because she gave me my sanity back and brought love back into my heart again. There had been so much hate and bitterness; all I ever wanted was to know who had killed my child and where they'd left his body. Laura brought love back to our hearts again; she's twenty-one now and studying at Queen's.'

The fact that Margaret and her family did not know where Brian's body lay made the grief all the more difficult to come to terms with. That they did not feel free to speak openly about his disappearance did nothing to help their situation either. 'I couldn't tell my story all those years,' says Margaret. 'I felt terribly intimidated. It was only with the IRA ceasefire in 1994 that I got the chance to tell my story. I told it first to one newspaper and then all the different papers caught onto it. It was such a relief to be able to talk after all those years. At first it seemed to be just me telling this kind of story, but then Jean McConville talked about her mother, Liz, and then other people came forward. We'd been left all those years with nobody or nothing to turn to. People couldn't believe it when my story appeared on television and in the papers; some of the neighbours came crying to my door, apologising, because they'd heard that I'd been in contact with Brian all those years.'

Out of the blue Margaret received a letter from WAVE Trauma Centre, an organisation set up in 1991 to support people bereaved and traumatised in the 'Troubles'. She hadn't heard of them before. 'At first I didn't see how they could help because all I really wanted was to have Brian back,' says Margaret. 'Eventually I did go to the centre, though, and it was the greatest thing I'd ever done. I found it was a help because there were other people there who had lost loved ones too. It didn't matter what religion you were – nobody cared – and you just sat and talked. It was the first time I was able to laugh without feeling guilty. Or I could sit and cry, it didn't matter. I just felt so much relief; it was wonderful.'

In 1998 Margaret was one of a group from WAVE who went to the White House at the invitation of President Clinton. While waiting to go into the Oval Office a man approached her, enquired was she a member of the Irish group and then proceeded to ask what WAVE was all about. 'When I told him, he asked if anything had happened to me. I told him my son was taken away by the IRA and murdered and that now all I really wanted was to have his body, so that I could put it to rest before God called me home. I told him it was a long story and that I knew he wouldn't have time to listen, but he pulled up two chairs and I was able to tell him my story from beginning to end. He was the most wonderful man and I will never, ever forget him. He gave me his card and it turned out he was the President's special adviser, Jim Lyons*. So I couldn't have spoken to a better man!

'We were about an hour in the Oval Office and President Clinton was really lovely. When we were leaving he came over and put his hand on mine and said, "I promise you I will help you find your son." I believed him; and ten months later Gerry Adams came to see me, even though I'd already told him my story two years earlier. At the time he'd looked into it, but had come back and told us that it hadn't been the IRA who had taken Brian. I'd told him it might not have been sanctioned by the IRA leadership, but that I was sure it was IRA men who had taken it upon themselves.'

Clinton must have put pressure on Gerry Adams, however, because within a year of her visit to the White House the Sínn Fein leader came to tell Margaret that she would get her son's body back. 'I can't describe how I felt to hear that,' she says. 'There were tears and I was speechless. I couldn't believe it! Right enough, a dig started in a field in Colgagh, Co. Monaghan and the Gardaí dug there for six weeks from seven o'clock in the morning until ten o'clock at night seven days a week. We went down a couple of times a week; I'd have stayed all the time, if I could have. The Gardaí were so, so good, but they gave up one day because it seemed there were no bodies to be found. Within about ten or fifteen minutes of the dig being called off the Gardaí went to a part of the field where they hadn't dug because the powers-that-be had said that the information they'd received didn't indicate that the bodies lay there. Within the first few shovel fulls of digging Brian was found, along with the other lad who had disappeared at the same time. That was on 29 June 1999. And so God came back into my life that day and it was fantastic because for all those horrendous years I thought there couldn't be a God.'

The bullet that killed Brian was found in the grave. 'It seemed the IRA men had walked him to the spot with his hands tied behind his back,' says Margaret. 'So he must have known he was going to die. Following the inquest he came home on 1 September and we laid him in front of the living room window until 4 September when we had a lovely funeral service for him in St Teresa's Church. We go down regularly to Colgagh; the Gardaí put a massive big rock near where he was found and we've put a photograph of Brian there and a plaque thanking the Gardaí. The farmer who owns the field told us the land will never be used for any purpose and we can visit any time. It's so peaceful there and the wee birds are always singing. Getting the body back gave a kind of closure because I used to go to bed at night wondering where his body was; that was always my last thought at night and my first thought in the morning.

'After the ceasefire we'd put ads in the papers asking for information. One person who rang and gave an IRA code-name said Brian was buried up the Glen Road under some steps leading to a housing estate; the police had spent a whole week digging, but there was nothing there. That shattered me completely because I'd been so sure that they were going to find him. We even bought his grave in Milltown Cemetery. So it's made such a wonderful difference to us having a grave to visit and I thank God that we have our lives back now. I can feel Brian's presence sometimes and when I think of all the years I'd lost God and now I know He's with me, too. But I still sit and wonder sometimes why they left him all those years? He'd never, ever done anything. I feel I do need some answers from the IRA.

'WAVE has done so much for me, though. It was through them that I got Brian back and that's why I'm happy to do voluntary work for them now. I answer the phones and I go out with the other outreach workers to visit people who have also lost loved ones. Sometimes people's hearts are breaking and they ask if anything ever happened to me, and so I tell them about Brian. It helps them to know that they are not alone in their suffering and, for those with graves to go to, it's a comfort to them to know that they have a grave to visit whereas I had nowhere to go to for twenty-one years. I like to listen to people because I was denied that for so long; I know what it feels like to want to talk. I will never, ever tire of telling my own story; as long as I live I will keep talking about Brian because I couldn't talk about him for all those years. That was the worst part of it – having to bottle it up. It was too hurtful even to talk among ourselves; we couldn't even have a picture of Brian up because I couldn't bear to look at him when he wasn't with us. I used to keep his pictures on top of the wardrobe and I'd take them down now and again and just sit and sob my heart out. But when the ceasefire came and I started talking about it I was able to put the photographs up again. They're everywhere now.

'I will do anything I can for WAVE. I used to go up every day, but I don't always get there now. When I'm not well and I don't get to the centre as much it plays on my mind and I feel lost. They've done so much for me and it's become a part of me. As long as I'm on this earth I will stay involved with them because I simply can't imagine living without them. It's just something I need to do.'

The last contact Mags Riordan ever had with her son, Billy, was an email she received from him when he was visiting Malawi in February 1999. He was staying in the remote village of Cape McClear which he had visited twice before and loved so much that he had decided to go back again. In the email he urged Mags to go there sometime, describing the place as 'paradise'. Since then Mags, who lives in Dingle, Co. Kerry, has indeed visited the village – fifteen times, in fact, although not in the kind of circumstances that her son could have possibly envisaged. Two days after he sent the email Billy went for a swim in Lake Malawi and never came back. He was an experienced swimmer and diver and his friends on the beach heard no cries for help, so Mags can only imagine that her son must have 'gone down like a stone', if he didn't have time to call out or hang onto a nearby boat. A post-mortem was never carried out, but Mags reckons it must have been a brain haemorrhage that took her twenty-five year old son. 'I'll never know what happened in the water that night, but obviously it was something drastic because he went down only about twenty metres from the shore,' she says. 'I've always suspected it was a brain haemorrhage because apparently you just go down like a stone. So basically he'd have gone wherever he was at that time.'

Mags first went out to Cape McClear twelve months after Billy's death and she placed a memorial stone with the inscription 'This is paradise' beside the beach. It was 'very tough' being there at first, but it did not take long for her to come to appreciate her son's description of the place and she ended up staying for a period of three months. 'Lake Malawi is absolutely beautiful,' she says. 'It's massive – the size of Holland – and so you can't see land on the other side. There's a long sandy beach with trees and the water is lovely and warm. It's just gorgeous. Malawi is known as "the warm heart of Africa" and it's very, very true; the people are very friendly, helpful and hospitable.'

Cape McClear made such an impact on Mags that she went out two more times that year – once in July, the other at Christmas. She made another three visits the following year, during which time she decided she was 'going to do something' to help the villagers, although she was not quite sure exactly what that would be. As a teacher, she was appalled at the education levels in Malawi: only five per cent of girls go to second level school and seven per cent of boys, with a tiny 0.1% making it to third level. Primary level education is free but, having said that, there are only five teachers for Cape McClear's 1,500 primary school children. 'They have no books, no desks, no equipment and no pencils,' says Mags. 'They have nothing. With that in mind I went back in 2002 and brought out sixty kilos of books, and I spent three or four months in the school, trying to teach. On the first day I was presented with a class of two hundred and thirty children, but I said that was ridiculous and so we broke it down and I used to take groups of twenty-five.'

During that time the school had to be closed for several weeks because a maize shortage had resulted in a famine. 'People were literally dying on the village streets and the children didn't even have the energy to walk up the hill to school,' says Mags. 'I was part of a group that organised to bring food into the village and so we fed up to a thousand kids a day with likuni pala, which is a kind of porridge. The famine had just really kicked in when there was an outbreak of cholera and people were already weakened from the famine; their immune systems wouldn't have been great, anyway, because their diet was so poor, and so people were literally dying within eight or ten hours of getting cholera. I asked some medics what is needed to treat cholera and they said that it is eminently treatable – that you just need a saline drip and doxycycline. In fact, in a lot of cases you don't even need an antibiotic because if you just have a saline drip and you let the cholera run its course and they rehydrate then they're fine. I thought, "This is ridiculous – all these people are dying because they don't have access to basic medicine." I also found it unacceptable that in 2002 kids were dying after they'd had a bad cut – they'd get septicaemia and die two weeks later because they had no access to antibiotics. People just got better of their own accord or they died. So I decided there was not much point in doing something for the school if the kids are going to be dead before they get there and that's how the idea for the Billy Riordan Memorial Clinic came about. I came home in May and told everyone I was going to build a clinic in Malawi and they thought I had finally lost it!'

The people of Dingle cannot have been altogether surprised by Mags' announcement because they already knew that she was not the kind of person to sit back and do nothing. The endless TV reports of the horrific scenes in Bosnia in 1995 had prompted her to seek the help of her local community to fill a forty-foot container with food, clothes and medicine. In fact, together with her friend, Ann-Marie O'Connor, she did such a good job motivating people that three containers were filled in the end. Over the next few years Mags made three visits to north-west Bosnia to oversee the distribution of aid and to see for herself the horrific conditions in which people were having to live. She saw people living in houses with no roofs, doors or windows and with no form of heating in places where the temperature dropped as low as -30 degrees in wintertime. So her local community must have known that when Mags sets her mind to something that it *will* happen, no matter what it takes.

The first fundraiser for the Billy Riordan Memorial Clinic was held in Dingle in August 2002 when an evening of entertainment provided by an Elvis impersonator raised €3000. 'I thought, "Yes, this is it; we're on our way" and it just went on from there,' says Mags. 'I set a target of €100,000 and I said that when we reached that amount we would build; and so we organised a lot of fundraisers and got a lot of media coverage. It seemed to hover around the €75,000 mark for ages and I was wondering if we would ever reach our target when somebody sent me a card with a quote from the Dalai Lama written on it. It said, "When you think you're too small to make a difference, consider the mosquito." And I thought, "Yeah, OK. I've just got to keep going."'

It took just over a year to reach the €100,000 mark and the building work began a month later. Mags had already secured some land from the village chief. 'We had people claiming that the land the chief had designated for us was theirs,' says Mags. 'So we had to sort that out and then we had problems getting people to work and there were the usual problems of stuff being pilfered and sold. Access to the village is by one very steep dirt track and during the rainy season it was impassable for the trucks bringing building materials. We had a lot of minor skirmishes along the way, but the building work was finished on schedule in June 2004. If it had been done on Malawian time, it probably wouldn't have been finished for another year, but my American volunteer,

Dan Sansone, who runs a construction company in New York, took his New York building habits into the village. Malawians remind me very much of the Irish; they hang around and they wouldn't do a whole lot of work, but as soon as they're motivated they go like the hammers. I think the Paddies, when they went to the UK and to America, were the same: we went over with the name of being lazy, but when we were actually put in a situation we came up with the goods. These guys really were fantastic.'

A team of five Irish volunteers spent the summer getting the building ready for use. A carpenter, an artist, a student and two teachers painted, polished and mixed mortar in readiness for the grand opening, which had been scheduled to take place in mid-July, but in the end had to be delayed until 24 August. A twenty-foot container filled with furniture and equipment had been held up in a Mozambique port. A representative for the Minister for Health officially opened the clinic, witnessed by most of the village population, who had waited months in eager anticipation of having access to medicines 'for our children' so that 'they will not suffer or die so much'. Presumably they cannot thank Mags enough for the addition to the village. After all, until now they have never had a doctor or a nurse, let alone a medical centre, in their village. 'There hasn't even been any medication,' says Mags. 'There's twelve thousand people in the area and they have had nothing; this is the first time in their lives they actually have somewhere to go because until now they would have had to travel to Monkey Bay, which is the nearest town. It's only about twenty-five kilometres away, but it's over a dirt mountain road and in the rainy season it's very difficult to get over it. It's also very expensive. A round trip on the bus costs two hundred kwatcha – that's $2, but the per capita income in Malawi is only $150 a year. Apart from that, it is a government clinic and so when they get there often there's no doctor and no medication. Sometimes they went, anyway, in the hope of getting something, but at least fifty per cent of the time there was nothing there. It's very hard for us in the First World to imagine something happening to our child and literally having nowhere to take him. Or you take your life savings and you travel to the nearest clinic, only to be told,

"Sorry, there's nothing here" while your child is unconscious or screaming his head off with pain.

'Without wanting to sound too big-headed about it, I think the clinic is the single biggest thing that has ever happened to the village. It has to be! It means so much to these people that when their child falls and cuts his leg, instead of bleeding to death he's actually going to live because he's going to get antibiotics. We have set a token charge of twenty kwatcha to see the doctor and another twenty per prescription; the only reason we're doing this is because I think people have respect for something if they have to pay for it. The clinic is going to be so busy and the last thing we need is to have people clogging it up, coming when they're not really sick. If a situation arises where someone really can't pay we'll accept a couple of eggs or a cup of maize.'

The clinic has one senior clinical officer who receives a wage – Dr William Kizito from Uganda – but any other medical personnel are there on a purely voluntary basis. A GP from Dingle, Dr Paul Moroney, is going out in October 2004 for three months and Mags has other volunteer doctors from the UK and Holland lined up to go out in 2005. She has no fears about finding enough volunteers to keep the clinic running – doctors, nurses and administrative staff. 'I've no doubt I'll get people,' she says. 'There are so many people quite prepared to go out. When you ask someone to go to Cape McClear you're asking them to volunteer in a very beautiful place; it's not like you're asking them to go to a dust bowl in the middle of the Sahara desert. It's just gorgeous there and the people are so nice. It's a fantastic opportunity – they'll be living slap bang in the middle of a real African village and it will be a wonderful experience for them. Generally speaking, the medical people who have volunteered already have some African experience. Once you get to know malaria, meningitis, TB, bilharzia (which is the disease people get from swimming in the lake – it's a worm which infects the liver) and HIV problems, then really the rest of it is childhood illnesses, like chronic chest infections, worms and scabies. You also have a lot of children who have growth stunting because they haven't had a proper diet since the day they were born. I'm not a doctor and yet I can virtually recognise all those things now.'

One might imagine that now the clinic is up and running Mags will be content to keep it ticking over nicely. Not at all! Seeing how much more needs to be done in Cape McClear, Mags handed in her notice in August 2004 from her teaching post in Dingle so that she can concentrate full-time on further projects. The Gap, which was the backpackers' hostel where Billy, and later Mags, used to stay (even though it was 'in rack and ruin') is now being converted into a centre for volunteers. Also, a non-governmental organisation has approached Mags to see if she is interested in getting an irrigation scheme up and running in the village and the AIDS Commission has asked her if it can carry out HIV-testing and ARV (anti-retro viral) drug treatment in the clinic. 'I just realised there was no way I could go back to my job because there were so many things needing to be done in Cape McClear, if I just had the time to do them,' says Mags. 'I reckon it takes a week in Malawi to do what it takes a day to do here because, if I need anything, I have to drive to Monkey Bay, which takes three hours, and that's half the day gone. I'm up at six o'clock every morning and I'm going until five or six in the evening; that's literally how it goes.

'I would like to add an AIDS hospice onto the clinic – somewhere that people with HIV or AIDS can be taken and made comfortable, put on medication and then allowed back into the community. The AIDS Commission says patients should not be isolated in AIDS homes – that they should be taken in, put on an even keel as far as possible, and then released back into the village. So I'd like to build six rooms and get in specific AIDS nursing qualified people because I know these six rooms will be full at all times. The Commission estimates that forty-five per cent of the people in the village are HIV positive; and, even if they're only half-right, that is still a lot of people. It's in evidence all around the village – the number of people lying on the ground outside their huts, literally dying of AIDS. One girl has been there for the past six months and she's covered in bedsores, although it's really hard to know which are bedsores and which are the lesions people get on their skin in the advanced stages of AIDS. There are a lot of orphans in the village, but none are living on the streets because Cape McClear is a very tight-knit community and when someone dies there is always someone else to take care of their children. When I say that, very often they wouldn't be able to feed them every day, but the children would at least have a base. In the cities, though, you do see street children – hundreds of them.'

Mags no longer has time to teach in the local school, but The Billy Riordan Memorial Trust does sponsor bright pupils who wish to go on to second, and even third level, education. 'We currently have five students from the village in second level boarding schools and we have one girl at the Malawi College of Accountancy and a boy at the agricultural college,' she says. 'To avoid any scamming, I personally go and pay the school fees every term and buy the books. I would like to see the sponsorship scheme expand because in a country where so few go to second level, let alone third level, I think education is the basis for everything. Since Malawi became a democracy twenty years ago the country has gone to pieces, but how can you expect people who have poor literacy, no problem-solving skills and no mathematical ability to run a country? You can't!'

Mags has harsh words for the dozen or so organisations that have begun projects in Cape McClear and then pulled out – either because the scheme was scrapped or because there was not enough support or training given to allow the locals keep the project running themselves. 'There were two young people who came in last year and did excellent work – the girl set up a women's group, making skirts and bags, and the guy was doing an agricultural project. They left in May and the whole thing fell apart within a couple of weeks because the locals couldn't keep it running themselves. The organisation should have had somebody there for five years because you can't do something in one year or even two years. And the EU! The EU has spent €60m on building two hospitals in Malawi, but there are no doctors and no nurses to staff them. They built them and handed them over to the Malawi Department of Health but, as it is, Malawi only has forty per cent of the medical staff it needs to run what it's got, never mind two brand new 300-bed hospitals. Behind the hospitals they built ten fantastic villas for the medical staff and behind that there are eight more villas for the nursing staff. But there is no medical staff! The EU might as well not have bothered and it makes me very angry when I think how all that money could have been spent.'

Mags' remarkable enthusiasm about Cape McClear has brushed off on various members of her family. One daughter, Emma, has been out five times and her other daughter, Jennifer, has been twice. Two of her nieces have visited and her mother, Kitty Dillon, made her first trip in August 2004. Everyone who visits the village comes away deeply affected, it seems. 'Other people are impacted in the same way I have been,' says Mags. 'It speaks for itself when you go out there; it really does. We've learned far more from the Malawians than they will ever learn from us. Far more! I think probably the best lesson we can learn from Africans is that we need to go home and reflect on our own society. I find it more and more unacceptable each time I come home to see the waste in our society and to see how spoiled the children are here; the more I see that the more committed I become to what I'm doing in Cape McClear. There if you give a child a biscuit, instead of keeping it for himself he will break it in pieces and give a bit to everybody.

'I'm firmly convinced Billy was meant to die where he did because, if it hadn't happened there, this clinic would never have been built and these people would not be receiving the medication and the treatment that they're having now. Billy's death will save a lot of lives in Cape McClear, so I'm convinced it was meant to happen there. Absolutely convinced.'

Billy was not the first child Mags and her former husband, Richie, lost. Their first daughter, Niamh, died when she was only four months old; the brakes failed on the family's 'old banger' of a car. Mags was manoeuvring it on the Dingle quayside at the time and the car plunged into thirty foot of water. To this day, Mags does not know how she herself survived; there was no hope, really, for little Niamh when she became trapped in the bitterly cold water. Three years later their second son, Luke, died while he was also strapped in the back of a car. On that occasion it was a cot death. He, too, was only four months old. With Billy remaining as the sole surviving child, who can even begin to imagine what Mags and Richie must have gone through?

Remarkably, Mags does not consider herself to be particularly unfortunate. 'Sometimes I feel cheated – that it's all been very unfair – but I've never felt anger,' she says. 'Anger does no good to anybody; it just eats you up. I have been down a long, hard road and it's not finished – and it never will be – but, you know, the cup is either half full or half empty. There are lots of people who have had far worse lives than me; lots and lots of people. I see people every day in Africa and I wonder how they manage: I see people going through the most awful pain and suffering, people dying of AIDS and people who have lost their whole family to AIDS. And then I think maybe I didn't have such a bad time, after all.

'In Africa there's the poverty and deprivation on the one hand, but on the other side there's the huge richness of spirit that the people have. It's very hard then to compare the two societies. African society may be bereft of the luxuries and comforts of life, but they have a spirituality that we certainly have lost; and they have a sense of community, humanity and acceptance that we've lost. They have a sense of cheerful hopelessness whereby they are extremely cheerful, but they know that their situation is hopeless. They don't see a way out and yet they are so cheerful and so hospitable. I can't count the number of times I've been brought into a mud hut and given food I know should be going to the children, but I don't refuse it because that would be insulting. I would never eat my fill, though, because I know, if I did that, the children wouldn't get anything to eat until the next day.

'I started off doing work out there as a memory to Billy, but the more I get into it the more I realise I'm doing it because it's necessary and because I know it will make a huge difference to people's lives. I've discovered that it's not impossible to change things and I feel I owe it to the world to give back something; I owe it to people who weren't born as fortunate as me. It's very hard to go to Africa and not be moved: I just know I would not have been able to walk away from Cape McClear without doing something; I couldn't have because it would have haunted me. At the end of the day I know that what I am doing is the right thing to do.'

*Jim Lyons has kept in touch with Margaret, writing to her regularly, sending her 'a beautiful pair of rosary beads' and even paying a visit to her home during a visit to Northern Ireland with his wife, Marcia, in 2000.

Joey Dunlop

and The Lost Riders who followed in their hero's footsteps to bring aid to Eastern Europe

The late, great Joey Dunlop is a legend. There can be no other way to describe him. It was probably no surprise to his legion of fans across the world when at the end of December 1985 his name appeared on the New Year's Honours List: he was to be awarded an MBE for his services to motorcycling. This announcement came at the end of a year in which he had narrowly escaped tragedy in a boating accident, but went on weeks later to become the second rider in history to win three Isle of Man TT races in one week. Not to mention a fourth consecutive world championship!

No doubt many of his fans came in for something of a shock when their hero's name appeared in the New Year's Honours List ten years later, becoming the first motorcyclist ever to receive a second decoration from Buckingham Palace. He was to receive an OBE not just for his services to sport, but also for his 'humanitarian deeds'. Until then, most of his fans probably had no idea that the 'King of the Roads' was something of a hero off the race track as well as on.

Joey may have had nerves of steel when he was racing, but he also had a big heart. His widow, Linda, says that the only other thing in Joey's life, apart from racing, was his family and, whenever he brought his children on fishing trips to Donegal, he would always insist that any fish that were hooked were immediately released back into the water. He simply could not bring himself to kill them.

All in all, Joey made four relief aid trips to Eastern Europe, driving his old Mercedes van with a trailer behind – both packed full with food, medicine and nappies. It all started when the daughter of one of his neighbours, a young nurse called Siobhan Lagan, who was working in a Romanian orphanage, sent word home that the children were having to live on a ghastly ration of gruel, which was barely life-sustaining. She requested food be sent out from Northern Ireland.

Whenever word went out in the tightly-knit community of Ballymoney, Co. Antrim that Joey was planning a relief trip (after his initial visit to Romania, he also made trips to Hungary, Bosnia and Albania) donations would come pouring in. 'People brought everything to our house and the church hall and we packed it all for the journey,' remembers Linda. 'It was very exciting to see if you could fill the van and trailer; and it was good because you knew people were going to benefit from it.'

Once everything was packed Joey would take off, on his own, returning home between three and six weeks later, depending on how long the trip took. 'When he went the first time and he saw what it was like out there it prompted him to make more trips,' says Linda. 'Many's the time I thought he was a bit mad making the trips on his own, but I was more worried for him than anything else. You'd be scared that people would try to steal the food and so Joey always slept on a plank of wood in the van. Often he'd be stopped in the middle of nowhere and it would have been cold; on the first trip the diesel froze, it was that cold, but he still slept in the van! Joey was a very, very quiet man, but because he was on his own he had to speak up for himself whenever he came to a border crossing; the longest he ever got stuck somewhere was ten hours. He always brought motorbike stickers with him and gave them to border guards.'

Joey never spoke to the media about what he was doing, so it is little wonder that his fans were surprised to hear the OBE announcement. 'It wasn't a publicity stunt,' says Linda. 'He didn't want people to think he was doing it for the glory and so he kept it very quiet. He would have told me wee bits and pieces because he would have been upset about what he'd seen and he'd have been really, really strict with our kids about finishing their dinner, after seeing children who had so little to eat. But he would never have spoken much to people about what it was like out there and he never took photos for the papers because he felt it would have been unfair on the children in the orphanages.'

Rev John Kirkpatrick, who was Joey's minister at the time, has been involved in the Presbyterian Church's work in Eastern Europe since the 1970s and because he had visited those countries and had contacts there he was in a position to help Joey plan his routes. Although they had 'a good understanding' of each other, Joey did not tell Rev John much about his trips. 'He just did it, came home and then got straight back into the mainstream of life again,' says Rev John. 'I do remember him telling me, after his first trip, that the children in the orphanages were fed the heads and feet of chickens; that would have been normal in that environment. I've no doubt the trips did impact Joey. He wasn't a hard person; he was very sensitive. He came from a background where there was no prosperity or affluence and I think people who have grown up in that have more of a sense of identification with those people and they tend to be able to understand them more. He was able to relate to people and, seeing those children, I've no doubt it had a profound effect on him.

'Romanians will say to you, "A lot of people come here once, but not many come twice." The person who really cares will say, "I'm prepared to walk a little of the journey with you" and the fact that Joey went more than once adds integrity to what he was doing. It's not something you would choose to do, and it's not something you'll be attracted to. It's not easy and it's not pleasant. Not so much the physical aspect of it really – people have done more physically arduous things – but if you're a sensitive person, like Joey, being exposed to the suffering of others, that's harder. He may also have been driven by his appreciation of his own family and thinking of what he had.'

Rev John, who has himself been riding motorbikes from the age of eleven or twelve, recalls that Joey was a somewhat irregular churchgoer when he first became the minister of Garryduff Presybterian Church in 1987. 'He did become quite regular, though, as regular as his career permitted,' he says, 'He invited me down to his pub on a few occasions to speak to the lads and answer their questions. I remember on one occasion I did that and they all came to church the next Sunday! Joey was not traditional, he had his own way of doing things, which was refreshingly different in many ways. He was a very private individual, who was also deep thinking, and we had a mutual respect for each other. He didn't want to be this hero-figure; that didn't sit well with him at all. He was quiet, unassuming and self-effacing and a wee bit bemused with all the commotion about him.'

Although Joey never brought home pictures of orphans or of other people he met, he did bring home realms of photographs he took of the war graves and former concentration camps that he visited. Linda lent these photos to the members of The Lost Riders Motorcycle Club when they decided to follow in the footsteps of their hero, arriving at Tallinn in Estonia – where Joey's life was so cruelly cut short on 3 July 2000 – in time for the third anniversary of Joey's death. The Lost Riders had helped out at Joey's funeral when up to 60,000 fans turned out to pay their last respects to their hero. 'The Lost Riders are a great bunch,' says Linda. 'Whatever they do, they do it with the best of heart, and I was all on for their trip from the word go.'

The Lost Riders Motorcycle Club started off in 1998 as a small group of enthusiasts, primarily from north Co. Dublin, although there are now nine hundred members all over the world. They marshal the Skerries 100 races and they raise funds for travelling doctors, the Injured Riders' Fund, the Joey Dunlop Foundation and various other causes. 'Basically we formed the club to put money back into motorcycling and to organise some charity events,' says club chairman, Joe Carey. 'The first big charity event we did was a run across Ireland and back and we raised IR£23,000 for Our Lady of Lourdes' children's unit in Drogheda. We did that following my son's cot death at eight weeks, which happened six months before Joey died. We swore we wouldn't do charity fundraising again, though, because when we went to purchase the machine that they wanted to save kids' lives with the government charged us tax on it. That really annoyed us because the government should really have bought that machine and they had the cheek to charge us twenty-one per cent tax on it. I swore I would never do a charity event in this country again and I haven't, apart from our annual Christmas trip to a centre for children with learning disabilities in Navan when we all dress up as Santa Clauses and pile up our bikes with toys and selection boxes. The kids go crazy; it's absolutely brilliant. We also do two events a year for the Injured Riders' Fund, which was set up years ago for the bereaved families of motorcycle victims.'

Linda lent The Lost Riders Joey's maps and photos, which came in useful when they were planning their trip. The idea had come about following a meeting around the time of the second anniversary of Joey's death when Joe said to a few of his fellow club members, 'Wouldn't it be great to follow in Joey's footsteps?' A number of people were interested and when they began to talk about it more they decided that they couldn't make a trip like that without bringing some relief aid. 'We couldn't follow in Joey's footsteps to Estonia and bring nothing with us,' says Joe. 'Initially we were just going to gather some kids' clothes and toys from our families and friends, but then we realised we really needed to bring nappies and baby wipes as well. We did a charity run to Galway and back to raise money, finishing at The Pavilion shopping centre in Swords. We set up a few motorbikes in the foyer, including the red one Joey won the TT on, and displayed a map showing our proposed trip. People started giving us nappies and baby wipes and the manager of the centre said he'd never seen such an interest in a display and that we could keep using the space for the next month. We penned in the motorbikes and left two empty shopping trolleys there everyday; and when we'd come back at the end of the day they would be full of nappies and baby wipes. We couldn't believe it! In the end we had enough to fill a forty-foot container and four vans. It was absolutely amazing.'

Twenty-one people took part in the trip, travelling on five motorbikes as well as in the four vans. They had reckoned it would take a week to get to Tallinn, but in the end it took a full ten days. They lost a lot of time at border crossings, where they were frequently forced to spend hours waiting until they were allowed to continue their journey. They had to wait an irritating eight hours at the Polish/Lithuanian border and an even more infuriating thirty hours at the Lithuanian/Latvian border. They had planned to visit four of the concentration camps they knew Joey had visited, but in the end they only made it to one – Treblinka. 'After going to one I have to say I'd never want to go to a second one, never mind a fourth one,' says Joe. 'We knew from Joey's photos that he visited at least one concentration camp on each trip and that he went to Treblinka twice, for some reason; I don't know why. His close friend, John Harris, would say that Joey was always perplexed as to why people could do such bad things to each other. My own personal feeling is that if everyone visited a concentration camp there'd be no more wars in this world because it's the scariest thing you've ever seen. Not that you see very much, but just to think that 800,000 people were massacred at Treblinka. It just defies belief how human beings can do that to each other. Joey also used to visit an old war memorial in the Isle of Man and he discovered an old war graveyard in Tallinn that not many local people knew of until he found it.'

When The Lost Riders finally arrived in Estonia they stayed at the campsite where Joey used to stay, 'for authenticity's sake', and during their four days there they visited five orphanages. The TV crew who accompanied them on the trip to make a documentary for the BBC was only given permission to film in one orphanage – the one which was in far better condition than the others. The staff there reminisced about the visit Joey had made some years earlier. The children, who were mostly under eight, were too young to remember Joey, but they were thrilled to be visited by The Lost Riders and shrieked with delight as they took their turns to sit on the motorbikes. 'The orphanage where we were allowed to film was more like a mansion than an orphanage; it was absolutely gorgeous,' says Joe. 'But the others we visited were just like you'd imagine an orphanage in Eastern Europe to be. I remember one kid had been fed bread and water all her life; she was eight, but she looked only about three years of age.

'It was very, very hard for us. Some of the people on the trip – I've known them twenty or thirty years and they're not emotional at all – but they took it very, very bad. You just wanted to bring the kids home with you; you really, really did. It was very hard leaving them. One of the saddest things was that there was a brother and sister who had been placed for adoption in different parts of the world – one with an American family, another in Singapore. I couldn't understand how somebody could make that decision, but the way the staff look at it is that it's better they have a home to go to rather than no home. We brought out about seventy wheelchairs and they'd never seen a motorised wheelchair before. There was this boy, Michael, who was in a converted pram, he couldn't push himself, he had to be pushed everywhere, and when we arrived he was a very, very sad child. But when we gave him a motorised wheelchair it was the best thing in the world; he was so delighted with it. The children in the orphanages were the most well-behaved kids and I absolutely fell in love with a gorgeous girl, Natalia, who reminded me of my daughter. My best memories from the trip are of the kids; they had tears in their eyes when we gave them rides on the motorbikes, they were so delighted. A number of the married couples in the club are talking about adopting children from the orphanage. It would be nice, you know.'

The day after they arrived in Tallinn, The Lost Riders went to visit the exact spot where Joey skidded off the race track on that fateful day in July 2000. 'It was very, very intimidating to see where he died,' says Joe. 'I just couldn't get over the amount of trees and I was shocked that other people hadn't been killed there because the road basically cuts right through a forest. Whereas at the Skerries' races bales of hay are placed in front of trees and lamp-posts, in this place you couldn't do that because there were trees everywhere; you just wouldn't have enough bales of hay to do it. There was a freak shower just before the race began and Joey lost control at the final bend. I'd seen a photograph of Joey lying dead among the trees in one of the tabloid papers a few days after he died; myself and the other bikers went mad and we haven't bought that paper since. To finally see where Joey lay dead that day was horrific. Absolutely horrific.

'Two days later, on the third anniversary of his death, we went back to the same spot and I read a poem I'd written about Joey. We had hoped to have a service led by Fr Tony Conlon, a biker priest who is chaplain of Beaumont Hospital; he had planned to fly out to join us, but unfortunately he had to cancel at the last minute. We needed to do something in Joey's memory and so I sat down for hours and hours at the campfire and wrote a poem about my memories of Joey, while I burned the midnight oil. It was a lovely setting because all the people I shared those memories with sat with me around the fire. I'm not a poet, but in the end I was quite happy with what I wrote...

I Remember 'Joey'
We remember cheers and shouts
At Black Dub and Bay Hill
And anxious moments waiting for the light
And we recall the 21st at Misty Mountain slopes
Told the tale of who would win the fight.

Could we forget a rainy day in June of '85
When in a rain-soaked senior race he flew
Our hero ran the gauntlet, on a flooded mountain course?

To TT '89 he came but didn't race that year
I met him after practice in the beer tent
We talked on nothing for an hour, before he had to leave
He left me stunned in silence as he left.

At the Ulster on a sunny day
His pride on fire, written off the year before
The yellow helmet stormed in first
to claim the formula 1
And gave Dundrod its greatest ever roar.

At Turnagroff in '96 on roads of melted tar
I saw the master show the 'Quack' way round
While younger riders wilted in the searing August sun
He rode the course he loved and won the crown.

At Skerries 1994 on the RC45
Against a number of nimbler bikes he fought
On tight and twistier narrow lanes more suited to a twin
He led, the big one never caught.

And some days that we don't recall
The times he stood up high
And took the honours, twenty-six in all
He well knew how to celebrate
He'd spray the bubbly wide
And smile the greatest smile of all.

And now the thing we always feared
Has come to us this day
His light has not come on, although we all wait
Joey's yellow helmet won't be coming around again
Past Bradden, Bray or down Keppal Gate
No more will we stare in awe at Begarrow on full bore
Or Glen Helen beating Radio TT
Or Rhencullen on the back wheel
flying through the 30 zone
It's never going to be the same for me.

In the beginning there were roads
And all of them untamed
God sent a quick King the roads to run

Joey came and conquered them all
God bless 'Yer Maun'
Rest now
Job done

Joey Dunlop 1952 – 2000
RIP

Joe was a fan of Joey Dunlop's from the first race he went to at Skerries, around the age of ten. 'I've gone for years now to all the motorbike races in Ireland and the Isle of Man and some in the UK and I used to stand there, watching Joey fix his bikes,' says Joe. 'Whereas all the other teams would have top mechanics he'd be on the grass with his bits laid out everywhere. He got to know my face, but it wasn't until his last few years that I actually spoke to him. Joey kept himself to himself; if he chose to spoke he spoke, if he didn't, he didn't. I witnessed several times at races when he'd be setting up his bikes for the afternoon – there'd be hundreds of people around and they'd all be looking at Joey working on his bikes. He'd be quite busy and one of his aides would come up to him and say, "Joey, there's some people who want an autograph." He'd look around and say, "I'm a bit busy now, you know." Then he'd take a second look and say, "But let the kids in." If he'd gone over to sign his autograph for an adult he would have been drawn into a one-to-one conversation, but he genuinely wanted to bring the kids in. I thought it was a great way to defuse the situation.'

Joe was not particularly surprised when he first learned of Joey's aid trips to Eastern Europe. 'That would be something he would do and I admired him even more for it – the unselfishness of the whole thing, that's what I liked about it. Joey never took from the world, he always seemed to give back, whereas it was only when my son died that I realised you can't take from the world all the time. With Joey it was different, he was always like that, it was in his blood. I've only become like that because of personal circumstances in my own life. I'd probably still be a selfish git if my son hadn't died, to be honest with you, but people can always change.

'When I first heard that Joey went to race in Estonia I was amazed, but I came to understand why he went: although he was known out there, he was never hassled. I suppose most big stars would revel in the attention they'd get after winning a big race, like the TT, but Joey didn't like that at all. He'd always load up the van and go away if he won something big – that's how he chose to get away from the press because he didn't like being the centre of attention. He never kept the winnings from the races he won in Eastern Europe, he would either take the money and give it to an orphanage or he would hand it back to the organisers and tell them to put it in the prize fund for the next year's race.'

As his fans have been aware since Joey received the OBE in 1996, there was far more to their hero than racing. Rev John says, 'I'm sure there are some people who say, "What I really admire about Joey is that he got to the top and he didn't think of himself; he used his position to think of others." But he didn't do it because he wanted to look well and get some reward; he did it because he cared about people. There are some people who, when they get to celebrity status, say, "Well, maybe I should put a wee bit back in." But Joey never saw himself as having celebrity status, anyway. He had an appeal to ordinary people and that's one of the very endearing qualities and attractive things about Joey's life – that he was an ordinary person who did something quite extraordinary. He was driven by the simple desire to respond to people who had a need. He led an inspirational life. However, his story doesn't have the happy ending that people would want it to have. But isn't that life?'

Joey Dunlop never wanted to be a superstar. Nevertheless, his yellow helmet and number three bike became synonymous with high-octane wins, and his racing record remains unsurpassed – twenty six wins in twenty five years at the TT races. And five times world champion. 'The greatest legacy Joey left behind was that he was the greatest TT racer of all time – there's no question about that,' says Joe. 'I don't know any other motorbike racer who could come last and still get cheered over the line, as if he'd won the race. No matter where he was in a race people just went crazy. It didn't matter whether he won or not – it was just the fact that he was riding.'

The Lost Riders' trip to Estonia in 2003 gave Joe further insight into the mind of Joey Dunlop. 'I just wish now I had gone on an aid trip with him,' says Joe. 'Not that he'd have let me! He was just a loner, you know. Having said that, I wish I'd taken more of an interest when he was making those trips. I now plan to go to the TT races every second year and to Tallinn every other year in order to preserve Joey's memory. The Lost Riders are hoping to sponsor a Joey Dunlop Memorial Race in Tallinn; when we have it up and running we'll advertise it in the press here because we hope to see thousands of people going over and treating it as their holiday. Each time we go out there we will bring something with us, if not a van load, then money.

'What more can I say? Joey was my hero. Full stop.'

Des Bishop

who uses a combination of comedy and his own experience to deliver cancer awareness and anti-drugs messages

When comedian Des Bishop discovered a lump he did what many people would do: he ignored it in the hopes that it would 'go away'. It took a few months before he finally plucked up the courage to get it checked out. An ultrasound confirmed his worst fears – he had testicular cancer. He was booked in for an operation the following Monday.

That Sunday evening he turned up at RTÉ Studios, as scheduled, to record the first episode of the satirical show, *Don't Feed the Gondolas*, which was to be broadcast the next evening. Following the recording he went straight to hospital to prepare for his operation the next day; he spent Monday evening watching *the Gondolas* from his hospital bed. A couple of days later, while he was recuperating in his cousin's house, a journalist from *The Evening Herald*, who had interviewed him the previous week, phoned him. He asked was it true that Des had cancer. 'I said yeah, and he asked me a couple of questions about it and then asked if I'd mind if he wrote about it,' says Des. 'I thought it would just be a few lines, so I said yes. Three hours later, however, my picture was on the front page beside the headline *Cancer Shock for RTÉ Star!* It freaked me out a little because it was just a real invasion; my friends were freaking, too, because the article made it sound like I was going to die.'

Four years on, Des reckons it was a good thing that his cancer experience entered the public arena. Since then, he has given numerous television and press interviews about his experience, with the express purpose of raising cancer awareness. After the initial few interviews, he approached the Irish Cancer Society, saying he was not particularly interested in publicity for his own sake, but that he was keen to help raise the profile of the organisation in any way that he could. So now, whenever he gives interviews, he always makes sure to mention the organisation.

'I've done loads of interviews, mostly around the theme of men's cancer awareness,' says Des. 'I never say no to the Irish Cancer Society. I did a free gig for them in Dublin City University when they were trying to get people to sign up for Daffodil Day: I did some comedy material about cancer, trying to motivate people to join the army of people selling daffodils. Two years ago I launched a Brown Thomas 'Tackle' fashion show, which was about men's cancer awareness, and this year I launched the Back to the Shop Floor scheme on Daffodil Day. Mostly, anything I do for the Irish Cancer Society is performance-based, but I also show up any time they need photos. My main thing is raising awareness, by using whatever little bit of profile I have to help them.'

Des was twenty-three years old when he discovered he had testicular cancer, which is not particularly young, given that it is most common in men between eighteen and thirty-five years. 'My whole mission is to get young men to check themselves and to get them more involved in getting health checks and screenings,' says Des, 'Because the only way you can die of testicular cancer is to be totally one hundred per cent ignorant, by completely ignoring a lump. Basically, it's the most curable form of cancer. My message is also to get men to talk more, to be more open with each other, particularly regarding health and hygiene. Men are men – I'm not trying to change them – but in terms of health and hygiene it's important. If you get a generation of men who are open about it, then when they get older and they get things like prostate cancer it just makes life a lot easier. Prostate cancer is more serious, it can't be cured, it can only be treated, but still you can live with it. It is very common in older men and people are probably more aware of it since Charles Haughey got it. And the more awareness there is, the less and less common it is that people die from it; Haughey goes on forever!'

The Irish Cancer Society can put people in touch with others who have experienced the same kind of cancer. When Des first contacted the organisation and was offered this service he chose not to avail of the opportunity because he already knew several other young men who had had testicular cancer. 'I had no questions at that stage,' he says. 'Testicular cancer is very curable and I had already had an operation; I'd also had radiation to ensure it wouldn't spread to my stomach. I didn't need the Cancer Society to put me in touch with other people. I'm now on the list, though, if anyone wants to ring and talk to me, but nobody's ever actually rung me.'

Shortly after his operation Des paid a visit to The Arc, a holistic cancer centre on Eccles Street. He only saw one other man; everyone else in the waiting room was female. 'I loved the place; I thought it was great,' says Des. 'But I didn't go back; I would have if there had been more men. But you see that's the thing: women are better at those types of things. Life is easier for a woman with breast cancer than it is, say, for a man with prostate cancer because women have so many support networks and there's so much awareness and so much information about breast cancer. That's why it is my mission to up the awareness about men's cancers.'

When Des discovered his lump he did immediately think it might be cancerous and he remembers what it was like to have this confirmed by the specialist. 'It's horrible when you find out; it sinks in and then you get all the information and it turns out it's not that big a deal. So you have half an hour when you figure you're going to die and then you just start to gather information. I told a couple of people and I had a good cry with them; then I got on with it. I didn't have to go ahead with *Don't Feed the*

Gondolas, but I decided I would; although I wish I hadn't. My heart wasn't really in it and I got a lot of flack from people because it was a bad show; and it was tough to be dealing with that as well as the cancer.'

Des reckons that, to a certain extent, cancer is still a taboo subject. 'The one thing I didn't like was everybody knowing that I only had one testicle,' he says. 'And that was a problem for a while. I remember one day I was walking down the road and this car sped past and the people inside shouted out, "We know you've only got one ball!" Now that really annoyed me; I wanted to throw rocks at them because I didn't like the kamikaze style in which they did it. I thought, "At least stop the car, get out the five of you and let me come back at you." I felt very low, but obviously that's faded by now.

'Part of the fear about testicular cancer is that you're going to lose your testicle. That's the big problem and that's the one thing you have to get over. It doesn't bother me today at all though, and my story is about how I'm cool with that now. I talk about it on stage – that it actually doesn't really matter. I have a whole twenty-minute comedy routine about getting cancer and I joke about having one ball. While there is a risk of it spreading into the lymph nodes of your stomach there's no risk of it spreading into your other testicle; I think that's unheard of. Your sperm count goes down a little bit, but they told me at the hospital that there was no need to go to the sperm bank. If you get chemotherapy you have to go, but I just got radiation (in my stomach, just to be safe).'

Des thinks the world of the medical staff at St Luke's where he received his radiation treatment; he even dedicated his DVD to the nurses there because he thinks they're 'the best'. Although it was released at the end of December 2003, they did not find out about the dedication until six months later. 'Better late than never,' jokes Des. 'They have also asked me to open the AGM of the Irish Oncology Nurses Association later this year, which I will do of course. I think nurses are the best breed of humanity, especially oncology nurses. It's a vocation, like the priesthood. A serious vocation.'

Whereas Des's work with the Irish Cancer Society is fairly high-profile he is also involved in other volunteer work, which he has never spoken about in public before now. He supports drug addicts who are trying to 'come clean' and he gives talks, well, gigs really, in prisons and areas of deprivation, like Ballymun in Dublin and The Glen in Cork city. Des himself lived in The Glen when he was studying English and History at University College Cork and it was in Cork that he took his last drink – at the age of nineteen. 'I drank too much and when I was drinking the problems didn't seem to stop, so it became very obvious that I just couldn't drink,' he says. 'So I stopped drinking and stopped getting into trouble. I don't touch a drop now. When I do anti-drugs gigs I talk about the benefits of not drinking and how my career has done well because I don't drink. It's all about letting people know that there is a life beyond drugs and alcohol because addicts do wonder what kind of life they will have if they kick the habit. There's no doubt they listen more to people who have had a little bit of history with addiction themselves.'

What kind of response does Des get? 'It's always good, but then I'm funny as well. Like when I spoke in The Glen I did a half an hour of material about living there. I always use my comedy. You don't go into Mountjoy without having your wits about you: I've been there a number of times and sometimes I bring other speakers with me. I've only been in the women's prison once and I found they were a lot harder to deal with; they appeared less inclined to admit their weaknesses. That's probably because women are survivors, they will not admit defeat as easily as men will, so women in prison are more likely to say, "I'm fine. I can get through this; I don't have a major problem."'

Des's work with addicts started when he moved to Dublin in 1997 and stayed with friends in Fatima Mansions who were also 'clean' and who were involved in the Rialto Community Drugs Team. He soon became involved, too. 'There's a drop-in centre for people, most of whom are on methadone, but some are still using heroin,' he says. 'It's just a place where people can come and get information. Basically they're a resource for the community, but their focus is mainly on people who have problems with drugs. They'll do things like help people get their social welfare entitlements; they'll also help get people on methadone or get them into drug treatment centres. They also run some courses, but most of them are gone now because the Community Employment schemes have been cut by Mary Harney.

'One time I did a *Who Wants to be Involved in the Community?* evening; it was like *Who Wants to be a Millionaire?* with all the different team leaders from the local community groups coming in to answer questions. It was to raise awareness in the community by getting all the groups together and encouraging them to work together more. Because I had a little bit of history myself and I got help I like to help others now. It's like you can only keep what you have by giving it away.'

Des no longer lives in Fatima Mansions, but he enjoyed the experience. He says, 'It wasn't like, "Oh my God, I've ended up in Fatima"; it was just that I was in-between places and I had friends living there who asked if I wanted to stay at their gaff. It was great because I wanted to see what it was really like, out of curiosity. I sometimes take their older kids to Trinity and tell them that's where they want to end up; I've also taken them on skiing trips to France. It isn't charity work; it's just a little bit of a mission of mine. I don't think I'm going to help in any way other than showing them there's another way, a better life. I had parents who, as crazy as they were, were always giving me opportunities. So I'd like to think that, even though it's going to be hard for them – as so many kids from Fatima end up in trouble at a young age – that they won't be as hopeless as they could be and they won't be as hateful at the world. They'll know there's other things out there. I don't know if any of it is sinking in, but the main thing I want to sink in is that, as they start to get older and start drinking, they can talk to me.'

Des himself was 'a bit of a wild kid' in his native New York, although he is quick to squash media reports that he was ever arrested or expelled from school. 'Looking back now, I was a kid who liked to drink when I was young and liked to write graffiti; that was the extent of my craziness. I started drinking at twelve, I was certainly wayward in that department, but I never got in trouble with the law. I just got in trouble at school. Queen's, New York was an upper-working- to lower-middle-class white neighbourhood and there were all these 'crews' or middle class gangs of young kids who thought they were tough. I was tied into no 'crew' really and I ended up in trouble with a couple of 'crews'. It was just kids' stuff, but it was serious at the time and I had a couple of people threatening me. I was really stressed.'

When Des turned fourteen a cousin in Waterford invited him to come and live in Ireland; his parents were reluctant at first, but they eventually agreed because they had become increasingly concerned about their son's behaviour, particularly his drinking. Des was enrolled in St Peter's, a boarding school in Wexford, and spent the weekends at his cousin's. He has never looked back. 'Ireland is my life now,' he says. 'I can't imagine my life without it. Obviously there's an element of slight tragedy, but it's not like I was happy at home. I've had so many different lives now: I was brought up in a quiet, comfortable neighbourhood in New York, I went to an agricultural boarding school with farmers' children in Wexford and I spent a year among the upper middle classes of Dublin when I repeated my Leaving at Blackrock College. And since then I've spent time as a 'ghetto tourist' in Cork and Dublin.'

Des further broadened his experiences in 2004 with his successful RTÉ series, *The Des Bishop Work Experience*. A striking mix of comedy and social comment, the programme saw Des, who has made a full-time living from comedy since 1999, give up four months of his life to work in minimum wage jobs as a hotel porter in Dublin, a swimming pool attendant in Tralee, a cashier and shelf stacker in a Dundalk supermarket and an employee in a fast food chain in Waterford. He experienced first hand the realities of living on the minimum wage. 'When we started work on the programme we obviously thought we were going to be crusaders for the minimum wage,' he says, 'But we discovered it's not that black and white.'

Was Des tempted to take any shortcuts during the four months? 'No, I lived for a month on each job, no messing. You know the way you say if you cheat you'll only be cheating yourself? I would love to have been able to cheat, but I couldn't; I would have been cheating myself. Besides, if I didn't have the experience I wouldn't have known what to say for the TV programme or the comedy show that resulted from the experience.'

Des reckons that the 'average guy' on methadone, alcohol or cocaine who may have 'stumbled across' *The Des Bishop Work Experience* would never have guessed that the man they were watching was clean and sober and living 'a totally amazing life'. 'They wouldn't know that,' says Des. 'If you showed them a room full of people just like me, clean, sober, happy, they wouldn't realise that they can have that too. My experience is that when they see someone they know who used to be an addict they say, "What happened to him? He looks very healthy".'

It goes without saying that an addict is far more likely to pay attention to a message brought to him or her by someone who knows from personal experience what it is like to struggle with an addiction. 'I think a person who says, "Look, this is what I did; and this is what I'm like now" is a lot better than somebody coming in and saying, "Well, we're going to use the personal development model." Theory is bullshit! To be honest, I resent a lot of the academic side of addiction because I think it actually ruins a lot of people. It takes a lot of people from the community who get clean and they go and study and then all of a sudden they get lost in the institutional side of it. I think you lose the personal touch then. The government-sponsored institutions, like Coolmine and Merchants Quay, aren't that successful; they do great work, but they're so hung up on the harm reduction model, which is basically giving addicts methadone and/or heroin (if they really get their way). I think that gives out the attitude, "Look, we know you're hopeless, so here's something better than hopeless". But that's not real life!

'I believe methadone is fine for temporary use, but that people shouldn't spend the rest of their lives on it. And I know that's happening. Without a shadow. I agree methadone is great for keeping crime rates down and that it's great for subduing a section of society, but I'm a real proponent of saying, "Get clean first and foremost". But I'm told, "Oh, but these people can't get clean". It's like, "What do you mean *these* people? These people are mostly from a certain type of area and all the people in that area are incapable?" That's bullshit! I'm surrounded by people who did get clean and who have totally changed their lives.

'All the people I know from places like Fatima, Ballyfermot and Ballymun who do get clean go on to have good lives. Not only do they have good lives, but they actually become quite successful, whether it's in the field of community work or just that they become really comfortable. It just goes to show that it's not about these people being capable; it's about them knowing that they can do it. I wish people would push that option more, instead of pushing methadone.

'The amount of people I deal with who go, "Well, the doctor told me that if I come off this methadone I might die". They put you on "maintenance" and then they put you on the slowest detox ever; and if you're detoxing over two years, within that time they're gonna use again. You've got to go speedy detox, sickness and then pain because the mind is too fickle; there'll always be a weak day when you'll have an excuse. So I encourage people to try and get clean: I tell them there's places they can go and that I'll support them. I also let them know that there's a whole life out there for people who are clean.'

Des knows hundreds, even thousands of people who have given up drink or drugs. 'I've been all over the world, as far away as Prague and Brazil, meeting like-minded people,' he says. 'And the problem is the same all over – addiction and alcoholism. I get sick of certain people who just can't get it together and eventually you have to draw the line. I just go, "Look, you know what to do; when you really want help give me a call". Some people don't want to get help and some people are very devious; that's just the way it is.

'I get more comedians ringing me looking for gigs than addicts ringing for support. I can tell you, people find it much easier to ring for a gig than to call asking for help. I'm still waiting for my first phone call from someone with cancer.'

Marie Devine

who strives to help people overcome eating disorders, just as she has done

Marie Devine not only began her life at forty. By turning her back on self-abusive habits she developed in early childhood, she also saved it.

She was five or six years old when she first adopted anorexic behaviours – eating very little, taking laxatives and making herself vomit – habits which years later resulted in a number of serious health problems. But it was only in 1995 when she was rushed to hospital after she collapsed getting into her car one day that she decided she must fight her eating disorder, if she was to avoid a premature death. 'It was like a wake up call,' she says. 'By that stage I had done a lot of damage physically. You name it, I had it: I had serious problems with my bones and teeth as well as my heart.'

Knowing it would be far from easy to change the habits of a lifetime, she started to attend Bodywhys – a group for people with eating disorders and, six months later, she checked into St Vincent's Hospital where she spent three months on an eating disorders programme. On leaving hospital she reckoned it was imperative to return to the Bodywhys group in order to keep herself 'on the straight and narrow'. It was therefore a huge disappointment to her when she discovered that, for various reasons, the group had disbanded.

'The eating disorders programme had been pretty tough – I'd had to eat 3,000 calories a day and I'd really needed to build up my self-esteem in order to cut the addictive behaviour,' says Marie. 'At that stage I didn't really need to work out the issues that had caused it, but I did need to sort out the behaviours. The first six weeks I completely messed about; I didn't engage in the programme at all and I was getting away with anything I could, like making myself sick and running away to buy laxatives. I was getting up to all kinds of things and breaking the hearts of everyone who was trying to help me, but after about six weeks I realised that I was wasting time and I needed to get my act together.'

The Bodywhys group had given Marie the impetus to undertake the hospital programme in the first place and she had looked forward to returning to the support group. 'It had been the encouragement of the people in the group which made me realise I needed to actually go into hospital,' she says. 'When I went to the doctor he'd weigh me and ask what I was eating, but the group was all about how I was feeling. It was completely supportive, which I thought was great.'

In February 1997, a few months after she had left hospital, the group reformed with Marie now taking on the role of facilitator rather than participant. 'Although I still had issues and I was struggling a bit, I was very well by then,' says Marie. 'A few of us got together and we got two groups up and running – one for people with eating disorders (which I facilitated) and one for their families and friends. It was important to have a group for them too, because it can be very hard for them; the behaviours around eating disorders can be very revolting and I know people who've told their partner or friend and they've said, "How can you do that? That's disgusting." People often find it very difficult to cope with.'

There are now half a dozen Bodywhys groups in Ireland – in Cork, Galway, Waterford and Limerick as well as two in Dublin.

The organisation has four paid members of staff and around fifty volunteers, some of whom facilitate groups while others work on the Helpline (which receives about two thousand calls a year) and the online support group, which operates via the website, www.bodywhys.ie.

Marie, who now considers herself to be 'completely recovered', has been the chairperson of Bodywhys since May 2003 and devotes up to twenty hours a week to the organisation. That's on top of a full-time nursing position and caring for her elderly mother, who shares her home in Leixlip, Co Kildare. She also does some work for the Carers' Association, leading workshops on issues such as bereavement, stress, communication, listening skills and practical caring skills.

Even though Marie has been well for some years now, she remains committed to Bodywhys because she has never forgotten the lifeline it provided her in her time of dire need. 'When I started to attend Bodywhys meetings it was like being able to breathe again – that's the only way I can describe it – being amongst people where I didn't have to explain my anorexic behaviours,' she says. 'Everyone else was the same and, no matter what stage you were at, you instinctively knew how each other was feeling. It was completely supportive. An eating disorder, whether it's anorexia, bulimia or binge-eating, arises out of some kind of stress and people use food as a kind of coping mechanism. It's very isolating, so it's such a relief to meet with other people who understand.'

These days Marie is involved in the administrative and PR side of *Bodywhys* as well as facilitating groups, which involves introducing a theme and encouraging members to explore various issues, like 'How do I tell my family?' She says, 'The group is always non-judgemental, it's a place to talk about feelings and we literally meet people where they are at. It's not about therapy or giving advice. Because I've had an eating disorder myself it means I know straightaway where someone is coming from. The issue is more about feelings than food; food is only the symptom and so we steer the discussion away from any talk about weight. People with eating disorders, particularly anorexics, are very sensitive, competitive people. If someone hears another person has reached a certain weight, they will think to themselves, "If she got to that weight, then I can too." We have candles, flowers and background music to create a relaxed atmosphere and we always wind down the meeting with some relaxation or visualisation.'

It is incredible how Marie has turned her life around, given that only a decade ago she was 'in and out' of psychiatric hospitals, being treated for depression and self-harm. Her children were taken into foster care and she was frequently in court, sorting out issues with her ex-husband. Her family had distanced themselves from her since she had confronted her father about the abuse he gave her throughout childhood. 'It was very hard to find the motivation to get well when everything had been taken from me,' says Marie. 'The medical staff had to motivate me to stay alive; I didn't want to be alive because I had nothing to live for. Everything was gone.'

While Marie was in St Patrick's she was treated by Dr John Griffin, one of Ireland's leading experts on eating disorders. Although he was well aware of Marie's anorexia, he reckoned there was no point looking at that issue until her depression and self-harm had been 'worked through'. 'I was grossly underweight at that stage and I used to cut myself to bits,' says Marie. 'It took an awful lot of counselling and psychotherapy and just being held where I was at. I had many friends who moved away from me, but there was one who ultimately believed I could do it. And I did. Eventually.

'When I was in hospital I made pottery figures of all the people in my life who had ever abused me or hurt me in any way. One day I went with a counsellor at Dun Laoghaire pier. I remember it was the most awful wild, wet day and I smashed the figures with a hammer and threw all the pieces in the sea. It was a very valuable experience, one of the most therapeutic things I ever did.'

It was around this time that Marie traced her eating disorder back to when she was as young as five or six. 'Although I certainly didn't have full-blown anorexia then, it was about that time that I learnt I could control my food: when everything else was out of control around me the one thing I could control was the amount of food that went in and out of my body. I discovered this by total accident one day when I picked up a packet of Saxa table salt off the kitchen table and swallowed it all. Of course, I got sick.

'I was physically, emotionally and sexually abused from as far back as I can remember and, as a child, I was powerless to stop the abuse. My family called me "the baby elephant" because I made noise on the stairs and "the dustbin" because I used to finish my sister's meals (the only reason I did this was to avoid the rows that ensued when she didn't finish her dinner; she was ill and had to follow a special diet). As I reached puberty I became terrified of how my body was changing (out of my control) and becoming more appealing to my father. I went to bizarre lengths to try and stop growing. I used to squeeze into a size eight corset belonging to my grandmother (she was four foot ten inches and I was five foot ten) and I tied bandages around my breasts – anything to avoid developing normally.

'When I started secondary school I told my mum I'd stay in school for lunch; I told the teachers that I was going home. In fact, I walked the streets, eating nothing and sometimes I collapsed in school and a teacher would have to bring me home. I was in and out of the old Jervis Street Hospital with all sorts of things that nobody could find any reason for and, by the time I was fourteen, I was attending a physician on a fortnightly basis for weight loss, constipation, panic attacks and a host of psychosomatic disorders. I was losing weight and every time I was weighed at the outpatients I was delighted when I'd lost another few pounds. It wasn't until I left school and home and started my nursing training that I learned about anorexia. From leaving school until my marriage began to deteriorate (when I reached thirty) I was very happy and I wasn't anorexic. I still had some of the behaviours, but I was well.'

With the breakdown of her marriage Marie's anorexia returned with a vengeance. Her weight plummeted, but she does not like to disclose by how much because she would not like anyone to take it up as a 'marker'. Suffice to say, she ended up looking like 'a stick insect'. 'When I looked in the mirror I was actually quite proud of myself – that I had bones sticking out – but I always thought my hips were huge and that if I could only lose a few more pounds I'd be happy. I was thrilled when I discovered I could fit into my daughter's confirmation clothes; I got such a buzz out of that.'

Marie has come a long way since the day she tried on her young daughter's special outfit and these days it's her commitment to helping others with eating disorders that gives her a 'buzz'. She is motivated by the belief that Bodywhys 'works' and she says that if even one person takes a step on the road to recovery as a result of what she is doing, then it will have been 'worth it'. She knows from personal experience that having an eating disorder is very isolating, but that Bodywhys can help people feel less isolated.

'There is virtually nothing being provided by the health boards and we fill that gap,' says Marie. 'There are only three public beds in the whole country for people with eating disorders (in St Vincent's Hospital), so if you live outside Dublin you have to go into a general ward, which is totally inappropriate. I know a teenager who was recently admitted to hospital down the country and she was put on a ward with, in her own words, "old ladies who were wetting themselves." Some children's psychiatric services stop at sixteen while adult services start at eighteen, so there's that whole discrepancy. We are currently looking at what kind of services we can provide for youngsters.'

Eating disorders have the highest mortality rate of any psychiatric illness – about ten per cent of people die, either from medical complications arising from the disorder or from suicide. Inevitably, several people that Marie knows die each year. 'You feel very helpless when that happens and very frustrated that something wasn't able to reach them,' she says. 'You just wish that something more could have been done. At the same time you have to move on to deal with the living.'

Marie now has plenty 'to live for'. She is on good terms again with her mother and her siblings (her father died in 2000) and, since her return to nursing in 1995, she has moved a couple of notches up the career ladder. But, most important of all, her children (now in their early twenties) are living at home again. 'We're a very close unit,' says Marie.

'Some people maintain that they're 'in recovery' rather than actually recovered. I maintain I'm finished, recovered, done it. I suppose that, because it was my coping mechanism for so long, it would be very easy to pick up anorexic behaviours again, but I think I have the determination not to go down that road. I know I'd get a buzz out of losing weight again, but I have two watchdogs (my children) who wouldn't take long to pull me up short if they noticed I was losing weight.'

Marie's health is pretty good, considering all her body has been through. 'The wonderful thing about the human body is that it can recover,' she says. 'I was lucky I didn't do any long-term damage to my kidneys or heart because, if you go too far, they can be affected. I did lose an awful lot of teeth, that is typical because frequent vomiting makes you more prone to infection and I got abscess upon abscess upon abscess. Also, I have brittle bones and some degree of osteoporosis; my hips are shot through – they will have to be replaced. I also have "intestinal hurry", which means I get an awful lot of diarrhoea – that's the result of using laxatives. And I'll always have the scars on my arms from cutting myself. At the end of the day I consider myself lucky, though, because I can live with them.

'If anyone had told me before I started out how tough the road to recovery would be I'd probably have just topped myself, but then I would never have learnt to appreciate and love life as much as I do now. I do love life – I've learnt to appreciate the little things – and I'm very passionate about Bodywhys because I know it can work.'

Like Marie, Joy Wall spent many years wanting to die. She developed anorexic behaviours during her early teenage years, although they did not become 'full blown' until she was about eighteen; people started asking why she didn't eat anything. She had 'very, very low self-esteem' while she was attending school in Wexford and it was only when she started third-level education at University College Dublin that her confidence began to grow. 'I started eating then, but in second year at college I realised there was something wrong,' she says. 'Because I was feeling more confident I felt I should be able to eat and yet there was a fear in me to eat that became more prevalent at that time. My mind was very confused; after years of the same behaviour I really wanted to die because it was so hard to live.'

Noticing the difficulties Joy was having with eating, her then boyfriend encouraged her to see a counsellor, which she did (albeit reluctantly). She built up a good relationship with the counsellor and made good progress, until, that is, one day when the counsellor informed Joy she could no longer see her because she was moving away from Ireland. 'Just when I was in the middle of really needing somebody like that,' says Joy. 'That set me back and I went to a couple of other counsellors, but I just couldn't do it. It was another year and a half before I found a counsellor I could trust again.'

Joy also attended several Bodywhys meetings and although she found the facilitators, Marie Devine and Barbara Doyle, 'very serene' she could not handle attending a support group at that time. 'My mind was just freaking out because Bodywhys was very peaceful and supportive and I just wasn't used to that,' says Joy. 'I wasn't ready to share with others; I felt very vulnerable and I wasn't sure I wanted to get involved at that level. I suppose I was kind of denying I had a problem.'

In the meantime Joy met a few other people with eating disorders and they formed an informal support network, which worked well. 'Initially I had anorexia,' says Joy, 'But for the last two years of having an eating disorder, as I was trying to get away from the anorexia, I became violently bulimic. I started cutting myself and drinking and taking overdoses; it was all so messy. It took two years to come out of that. When I was really messed up I felt I'd gone too far and I would never be able to get back. At the end of the day what really helped me was my family; having my mum there, when I was doing all those crazy things, it was like, "OK, I'll come back at some stage." And I did. People can stay in that state for a very long time, but I knew I didn't want to.'

In 2001, with a degree in sociology and archaeology and a Master's in sociology under her belt, Joy returned to Bodywhys where she was offered a year's research post looking into services for people with eating disorders in the Eastern Health Board region. Some months later she was asked if she would be willing to volunteer on the Bodywhys Helpline. 'At first I thought I couldn't do it because of my history,' she says, 'I thought I didn't have the skills, but I really wanted to help people and so I did some training. I'd already taken the odd call on the office phone and I felt I'd built up some experience and so I decided to go for it. You're not supposed to try and help people on the Helpline; you're just there to be with them. I enjoyed doing it and I suppose it confirmed in me that I was doing OK. I particularly enjoyed talking to the parents of sufferers; the parents often freak out more than the people themselves, who are often in denial. It's hard for someone with an eating disorder to feel that their parents support them one hundred per cent (as there are so many uncertainties in their minds) and are going to be there for them 24/7. I suppose if parents can just get that across to their daughter or son it's good.'

In June 2003, just when her life was running on an even keel, Joy suffered a 'pretty severe' stroke, which completely changed her life. She was only twenty-seven years old at the time. She couldn't speak or walk, although she made a fairly rapid recovery and was walking again within a few weeks. Her speech took some time to come back, however, and she still experiences difficulty at times finding the right words.

On a more positive note, the stroke had an extraordinary side effect. 'Since the stroke I've got over all those hidden things that I thought I'd have for the rest of my life,' says Joy. 'Even though you mightn't be active in your eating disorder – you mightn't vomit or starve or cut – you'd still know "I feel fat" deep down. But that feeling has completely gone. It seems the stroke has wiped away a lot of things, which is great. It's given me a different perspective on life and I've really had to reassess things. I'm pacing my life much better now: I used to push myself by working a stupid number of hours a week, but I wouldn't do that now. I've moved back to Wexford with my boyfriend, John, which we should probably have done a long time ago. We are building a house and hopefully we're going to get married.'

After her stroke Joy was unable to return to work, but Bodywhys gave her the opportunity to regain her confidence in the workplace by offering her volunteer work, which she could tackle at her own pace. 'It was great because it was very flexible and I only went in if I was feeling up to it,' she says. 'It took a few weeks to get my confidence back, but then I was grand. Initially I did simple things like photocopying and then, after a while, I wrote some articles for the newsletter and I worked on the database. It was pretty simple stuff, but they gave me the time to do it and it was fun. The Bodywhys office is great – it's a very healthy, supportive environment and, I suppose because of the nature of the organisation, it's always very centred and calm. I miss it since I've moved to Wexford, although I'm currently helping them with small pieces of research.

'My mum thinks the stroke was a good thing because I've been so much more relaxed since I had it; and I agree with her. My mind used to be so messed up, but at least I can say now that it's under control, I'm happy and I don't want to die anymore. I spent so many years trying to die, but now I'm afraid to die because I'm enjoying life so much. I've so much to look forward to; I'd love to continue doing research on eating disorders. And I can't wait to have babies!'

Richard Donovan and Mark Pollock

who have run marathons all over the globe to fundraise for their favourite charities

Irish charities simply would not be able to function without the tireless fundraising efforts of their supporters. Sales of work, flag days, church gate collections – there are many and varied means of raising money for organisations – and most Irish people, at some time or other, have probably turned their hand to at least one of these activities; perhaps they have shaken a tin for their favourite cause or participated in a sponsored fast or walk.

There are some people, however, who go to quite extraordinary lengths in order to fundraise. In 2002 Galway man Richard Donovan ran an ultra-marathon on all seven continents and at the North Pole to raise funds for GOAL and the Galway Society for the Prevention of Cruelty to Animals (GSPCA). Mark Pollock from Holywood, Co. Down ran the Gobi March, an arduous six marathons in seven days, in 2003 and the North Pole Marathon in 2004. No mean feat for someone who is blind and literally cannot see his next step! Sight Savers International was Mark's chosen charity.

Richard's achievement came about following the death of his parents. He and his brothers, Paul and Gerard, had run the Marathon des Sables in 1999 in memory of their father, Paul, who had passed away the previous year. Paul had been one of the founding members of the credit union movement in Galway and a fiery campaigner for the rights of the underprivileged, exposing himself to threats and abuse in the 1970s when he put pressure on Galway City Council to house Travellers who wanted to 'settle'. It was following the death of his mother, Mary, in June 2000 that Richard decided to undertake another challenge, this time by himself. 'It was 2001 before I hatched out the plan to run an extreme race on each continent, taking in snow and cold, heat and altitude,' says Richard. 'I was a bit naïve, I suppose; at that point I was about three stone heavier than I should have been, but I started training in May of that year.

'I wanted a challenge, I wanted to do something in memory of my mother and I also wanted to do something to help the GSPCA. Both my parents were animal lovers and I was brought up with the idea that animals are as important as people; and I always thought the GSPCA had been low on the pecking order of charities because their work involved animals. I chose GOAL because my mother had always been an avid supporter and because of the organisation's association with sport. I wanted to do something for kids in the Third World, anyway, I suppose because they're the weakest section of society. I used to tell people that although what I was planning to do sounded extreme that at least at the end of each race there would be a finishing line; whereas there's no finishing line for kids in poor countries or for abused animals. I know the GOAL representative in Galway, Ronan Scully, really well and I've always admired him; I've also always admired the amount of work the GSPCA people do. They're utterly devoted to the cause.'

Richard started training 'quietly', only telling a few people of his plans; and his wife, Caroline, was supportive from the word go. By the end of the summer he was running over one hundred miles a week, as well as paying regular visits to the gym and doing some cycling. He started to plan his itinerary for the following year, trying to find a race that would capture the spirit of each continent, and when he heard about the South Pole Marathon he 'threw his name in', promising the organisers he would come up with the $25,000 entrance fee (although he had no idea how he was going to do this)! 'Come December I still wasn't firmly in the South Pole Marathon because I was still desperately seeking sponsorship,' says Richard. 'Eventually Accenture in Dublin came up with something and I financed the rest myself. So at the end of the year I headed to the South Pole and I ended up being stuck in the Antarctic for almost a month: the race kept being put off because the weather conditions weren't good. Basically I arrived down there with no CV of running behind me, but I was really fit, I had been running three hour marathons easily in training, so I knew I was in good shape. I injured my knee while we were waiting around to get to the pole and, as a result, I was given zero per cent chance of winning the race by a German orthopaedic surgeon who happened to be down there climbing a mountain. In fact, my knee was so swollen he said I had very little chance of even finishing.'

The race finally took place on 21 January – the first ever marathon to be held in the highest, coldest, driest, most windswept place on earth. 'As soon as we started the race I was hurting,' remembers Richard. 'I'd never experienced anything like it. I had never been in cold before, I'd never been at altitude before, and there I was running in wind chill temperatures of -50C at an altitude of almost 10,000 feet. You know when you see a film of people in space? Well, that's what it felt like to me (from what I imagine it to be like). I was in running motion, but everything was slow, so the pace of the race was phenomenally slow, even though we didn't realise it at the time. And the effort was enormous! It's the only race I've ever run where I basically suffered from the moment I started; there was never any kind of a comfort period. I just got on with it, though, because I was very determined: if you're doing something in memory of someone you push yourself along.'

Richard took lead position after the first six miles and did everything he possibly could to open up the gap he had created.

'Everything you wear when you're running inhibits your breathing,' he says, 'So I took my goggles off and pushed the face mask off one side of my face to help me breathe better, but there was a constant wind blowing and I ended up getting wind burn. That's where the naivety came in because I got snow blindness; I could still see, but my eyes grew red and very sore.'

Conditions were perfect for the first few hours, clear blue skies, and Richard managed to open up a huge gap. He knew this because the driver of the support snowmobile, which was keeping an eye on the competitors, told him he had a lead of over two miles. However, with less than three miles to go until the end, the weather changed and all of a sudden Richard could no longer see the next flag. 'Everywhere suddenly became grey and I couldn't see a thing,' he says. 'I couldn't see where the next flag was, even though it was probably only fifty metres away. I was essentially lost and I ended up running the wrong way: it seemed like a long time, but it may have been for only ten or fifteen minutes. It was a constant battle for energy and I remember thinking I was in trouble. My thoughts went from, "Oh no, the other guys are going to catch me" to "Oh no, I'm in trouble." I was getting more and more concerned, but with a strange yet scared calm, and I was aware that my life was potentially in danger. It was very sobering and I remember thinking with clarity that I should have taken out life insurance. However, the sky suddenly cleared and I did a full three hundred and sixty degree turn, looking for a flag. I saw something glisten in a completely different direction than I expected and I headed towards it. I came across the next marker, which turned out to be two miles from the end, and soon I could see the South Pole looming.

'As I was running the last few hundred metres I took off my head gear completely because for some strange reason I thought people wouldn't believe it was me! I felt this sharp ping in my ear, it was a little bit of frostbite hitting me straightaway. It's very hard to gauge distance in those conditions and I thought there was maybe a hundred metres to go, but it was really three hundred. And at the pace I was going, it took a long time to get there! So all the guys from the South Pole station were standing there, watching this guy coming in, with no headgear on at all, and they were wondering what the hell I was doing. It had seemed logical at the time to take off my balaclava! What had happened was I'd got a bit of hypothermia while I'd been hanging around, trying to find my way, so I was hypothermic, although the visible signs, like uncontrollable shaking, didn't hit me until just after I crossed the line. I've heard since that hypothermic people often make stupid decisions, so although I thought my thought processes were perfectly fine during the whole race, obviously they weren't. I remember at the time thinking quite clearly, "These guys aren't going to know it's me". And yet there I was with an Irish flag on my jacket! I was completely exhausted after the race, which I completed in a time of eight hours and fifty-two minutes, and I was on a drip for a day or so afterwards. I also had frost nip to my fingertips, where they went white, and I had some minor frostbite to my toes, basically the nerves in my toes went completely numb for a few weeks. But was it worth it? It sure was!'

On his return from the South Pole Richard had planned to compete in a race in New Zealand, but with no feeling in his toes he had to cancel. He rested for a few weeks before heading to the North Pole where he ran a solo marathon, becoming the first person ever to complete a marathon at both poles. 'There's no altitude there, so I was able to run it in less than four hours,' he says. 'I'd heard about all kinds of nightmare scenarios about falling through ice because you're literally running on thin ice above 12,000 feet of Arctic Ocean. And so each step was completely and utterly into the unknown.'

The next race Richard ran was the Poor Man's Comrades Run in Australia, which is basically a fifty-five mile uphill race from Sydney Opera House along the Old Pacific Highway to Gosford. 'I picked that race because it was advertised as 'no fees, no prizes, no aid, no wimps,' which I thought signified the Australian concept of low-key,' says Richard. 'It was a great race in terms of its camaraderie. I ran most of the time with an Australian ultra-marathon runner, Kieron Thompson; we chatted most of the way and the competitive element had gone by the time we reached the end, so we crossed the finish line together.'

In August Richard headed to South America to take part in the Inca Trail Marathon, which goes through cloud forests and over high mountain passes on the ancient highway of the Incas. The race distance of 27.5 miles barely qualifies as an ultra-marathon, but the terrain, altitude and ascent make the event extremely challenging (most hikers take at least three full days to complete the route). 'It was a tough race, but one that I enjoyed immensely,' says Richard. 'Peru is a great place; the people, the scenery, the trail itself, the whole experience was brilliant. It was undeniably hard, though, because you had to run up to 14,000 feet, which in terms of altitude is halfway up Everest, I guess. The sheer altitude coupled with the uneven and steep steps that characterise the Inca Trail reduced my breathing to short, loud gasps and wheezing. On many occasions my hands were clasped fast to my thighs as I literally attempted to pull my legs up over the steps. I was in good shape, though, and after a leg-wearying five hours and fifty minutes I reached the finish line in first place.

'I then ran the US 24-hour Championships, which means you run as far as you can in 24 hours around a mile-long loop. I went into the race hoping to beat the Irish one hundred mile record, so I was basically using the championship as a means to another end; I wasn't in it to run for 24 hours. Unfortunately, the weather was unseasonably hot, almost ninety degrees with high humidity, which wasn't very good for endurance. Most competitors, as I did, experienced severe cramps and dehydration because we just couldn't replace the fluids as quickly as we were losing them. It was simply too hot for records, so I made a strategic withdrawal after seventy miles when I knew the chance of a record attempt was fading. It's tough running the same course over and over, but you've got to look at these things in a certain way, and the way I look at them is that it's an experience that toughens you up. You have to try and make yourself enjoy the fact that you're suffering through it because it's only temporary and it does make you mentally strong (or it can destroy you)! It was the one race I did where I could dictate my own distance and still be a finisher, whereas with the other races I was doing, if I didn't finish the race

I would be a DNF (Did Not Finish) and therefore I wouldn't have completed my task.'

The next race Richard entered was the Himalayan 100-mile Stage Race, a five-stage race that traverses isolated jungle and pine forests, crosses major rivers and passes through small settlements and villages on the India-Nepal border. The third day consists of a race called the Everest Challenge Marathon in which people who are not competing in the overall race can take part. Incredibly, Richard won every single stage of the race, including day three. 'It was a very tough race,' he says. 'On the very first day, which was twenty-four miles, there was a cumulative ascent of 10,000 feet. And that was only the first stage! You were always on an incline that day and then, for the other stages, you were running at altitude all the time. It was hard, but you can get into a winning mode. I was very lucky on the third stage to hang onto the gap I'd opened up. A few miles before the end I suddenly saw a guy wearing a foreign legion hat closing behind me and I was almost puking all the way to the finish because I was really running my guts out to get to the line before him. I just managed to hold on and I beat him by thirty seconds. Looking back, I think the end of that race was probably the most satisfying. At that point I felt that, because I'd won a race in the Andes and I'd won one in the Himalayas and I'd done both poles, in my own mind that was reasonably satisfactory.'

Reasonably satisfactory? Absolutely amazing, others might say! Deciding he had yet to run 'a really long distance' Richard headed off to take part in the Trans 333, an arduous 333 km race in the dry and uninviting sands of the Sahara Desert of southern Tunisia. 'I just wanted to do a really long race to authenticate what I was doing,' says Richard. 'It was rough: it was organised by some French guys and they don't mollycoddle you at all. It's in one stage, so it just depends how fast you get to the finish. They give you a week, but it took me just under three days. I did most of it in the first day and a bit, I was in the top five for the first 100 km, but then I was reduced to a bad hobble because of the blisters I had. I also got acute tendonitis around my ankle and shin; I didn't know your shin could swell so much. All I could do was treat the blisters as best I could, try to ignore the pain, and keep moving. A few of us ran off course into Algeria by accident and one guy was confronted by a gun; the course wasn't marked well, just pieces of ticker tape on the odd desert bush. Some of these were missing and I veered off course; it was only a minor thing, but it added distance.

'I took off my runners at a checkpoint because I thought I felt sand in them, but what I had felt was massive blisters bubbling up. I quickly put my runners back on and kept going. By the last night I'd completed about 280 km, but I was in bad shape between my blisters and my tendonitis; I was in agony with my ankle and my feet were bloodied from the grating sand granules in my shoes attacking my already blistered feet. But it was a particularly nice, bright night, the moon was out and, maybe I was hallucinating or something, but I remember thinking, "God, this is nice." But the next thing I could see something moving in the dark. I wondered what it was, thinking it might be some kind of goat, but in fact it was a pack of about twenty dogs. I was crapping it when they all gathered around me and started barking and growling. I thought to myself that this would be an ironic way to go, seeing as I was supporting the animal sanctuary in Galway! I looked around and, whereas usually you don't want to see the headlamp of another competitor behind you, I was relieved to see this guy coming, with a massive stick in his hand. The dogs backed off and we continued running. Other guys met the same dogs; they must have sensed we were limping! One guy ended up running the last 100 km with a camel bone he'd found, just in case he came across more dogs. It was a relentless type of race, I had to hobble the best part of a hundred miles because it just got worse and worse and I ended up coming 12th place out of the forty competitors.'

For his European ultra-marathon, Richard 'manufactured' a thirty-eight mile run from Killimor, where the GSPCA has its animal sanctuary, to the Cuba pub in Galway. It was a fun occasion. He had invited people to raise money and run a mile with him; and so he was accompanied by a diverse group of people, including doctors, DJs and businessmen as well as a soldier, a journalist, a bar owner, a hotel manager , and even a sponsored dog. Finally, at 3pm on 14 December Richard's year of adventure running came to a close with almost 1,000km of racing under his belt. He had succeeded in completing the first ever global 'grand slam' of marathon running, completing a distance of 26.2 miles or longer on all seven continents and at the North and South poles, often in extreme climatic conditions and circumstances. As well as winning four of the races, he also became the first person ever to run a marathon at the North Pole.

Richard, who incredibly describes himself as 'an average runner', roasted himself, froze himself and went to dizzying heights to help the disadvantaged. As a result of his fundraising efforts he was able to donate €10,500 to the GSPCA and a similar amount to GOAL, although he can't be sure how much money he raised exactly because some people chose to make direct donations. After all the blood and sweat, if not tears, that he had shed in the previous twelve months he was disappointed with the kind of money he raised. 'There was an awful lot of good will that year,' he says, 'But there's a difference between good will and translating good will into money. It was a very successful year in terms of raising awareness, but the one lesson I learned is that you cannot depend on people to go to a bank and hand in money; you really need to bring the bank to them. That's not a criticism; it's just to say that it is difficult. It was very hard for me to run, organise the trips and fundraise as well; and, if I was to do something like that again, I'd go about it in a completely different way. At least my activities resulted in press coverage and gave credibility to the causes I was supporting. I went into schools and gave talks and slide shows and these had a positive effect on influencing young people's views of the importance of treating animals with respect and helping poor people globally.'

It is probably fair to say that the course of Richard's life has completely changed direction as a result of his experiences in 2002. For a start, he no longer works predominantly as an economist, but as an adventure organiser. One of the events he has organised is the 2004 North Pole Marathon, a race in which Mark Pollock took tenth place. 'Mark is a really great guy, a joy to be with,' says Richard. 'To finish the race at all was an achievement for him; you wouldn't think he was blind by watching his graceful movement over the terrain. He was an inspiration to everyone.'

The date of the race, 10 April 2004, was significant because it was six years to the day from when Mark went blind. An operation to repair a detached retina in his left eye was unsuccessful and he had already lost the sight in his right eye when he was only five. However, the race became a turning point in Mark's journey towards accepting his blindness. 'The conditions at the pole were the scary part,' recalls Mark. 'I'd never experienced temperatures as low as -50C before and it was basically a competition against the elements. The competitors were there for all different reasons, some were having mid-life crises, some were hard-core adventurers who just love that sort of thing and then others, like myself (although I didn't realise it at the time), were trying to prove something to themselves. I was a little bit disappointed to take joint 10th place with my guide John O'Regan (there were fifteen entrants) and I asked myself afterwards, "Why am I here?" I decided it wasn't good enough to go to the North Pole just because I wanted to do a run or because Sight Savers would get some money out of it, if I didn't actually enjoy being there.

'After the race I had a discussion with one of the hard core adventurers, Sir Ranulph Fiennes, who came second place. He asked me (and I wouldn't have taken this off anyone else), "Why are you here? What are you trying to prove? Because it wouldn't matter what age I was, I would always want to beat you on this terrain. Why, if you want to do something competitive, are you running at the North Pole where it's difficult to run? If you want to be competitive, why don't you go and compete on a level playing field? And if you want to come up here because it's an incredible experience and you meet interesting people, well then enjoy it for what it is." He wasn't pulling any punches when he said that and I didn't necessarily want to admit that it had been difficult for me to run in soft snow where you have to jump over holes in the ice. I wouldn't have wanted to admit that it had been hard for me as a blind person, because I didn't want to admit that anything was difficult.

'Ranulph was basically saying I shouldn't have been disappointed that I wasn't as quick as he was; he then went on to say it was amazing I had got around the course at all. That conversation changed my view of the whole experience. It allowed me to say, "Well, that event was absolutely incredible: to do a marathon at the North Pole is just a phenomenal experience, never to be forgotten." I do like to compete, however, and now I understand that I need two strands to my sport. I have to have experiences, like the North Pole, which I can enjoy, and I have to have something else in which I can compete on a level playing field.'

As it happens, Mark was an international rower before he went blind and it is a sport he continues to do competitively, without being hindered by his loss of sight. In 2002 he won medals for Northern Ireland when he rowed in the Commonwealth Games and he continues to row competitively for the Lady Elizabeth Boat Club. He has also begun to look at other sports in which he could participate competitively. 'I've started swimming, kayaking and cycling (on a tandem) and some triathlons have a disabled category, so I would be able to compete on a level playing field in those. I'm also looking forward to doing some adventures, like a kayaking trip to South Africa.'

The first adventure Mark undertook was the Gobi March, an arduous six marathons in seven days across the Gobi desert in China, in September 2003. 'I was looking for a personal challenge,' says Mark, who little realised just how much of a challenge it would turn out to be. He trained hard for the event, running three or four hours a day on a treadmill with a fifteen-kilo pack on his back. So hard, in fact, that he 'overdid it' and, with only two weeks to go before the race, he found himself confined to bed with a temperature of 105F. 'I was in very bad shape, totally run down,' he remembers. 'I was completely out of action for four or five days and I was concerned I wasn't going to make it to China, which would have been a complete disaster.'

Although he did not complete any more training, Mark did make it to China in time to race. However, he and his guide, Nick Wolfe, came in for a rude awakening on the first day. They had been expecting to run on sand, but soon discovered that the Gobi desert is made up primarily of rocky plains with occasional rivers, bushes, cliffs and sand dunes. 'I'd say the first day of the race was probably the toughest thing I've ever done,' confides Mark. 'I couldn't believe it because I thought we were going to be running over sand, but there were rocks and bushes all over the place. Nick had to keep telling me when to step left, right, up, down; in many respects it was more difficult for him because not only did he have to deal with the strains of the event, but he also had to bear me in mind all the time and guide me. About halfway through that first day we actually had to go sideways along a ledge on a cliff face; there was a river running below us and Nick had the responsibility of making sure neither of us fell into the river and injured ourselves. We then had to climb up over the sides of the cliff and run across sand dunes; and by the time we got to the camp that night we were totally destroyed. I was almost a broken man. All Nick wanted to do was get his food and get to bed, but as well as that he had to make sure I was OK. I'd be calling to him, "Nick, Nick, can you take me to the toilet?" He was under serious pressure the whole trip.

'Basically the event went like this: day one was awful, day two was worse and day three was worse again. Day four stopped the rot, we began to feel we were turning a corner. And the strange thing was that on day five, when we had to run almost a double marathon, we got stronger and stronger. We just ran the whole way, feeling great! On the last day 10 km of the course was through a river; we were literally running along the river up to our knees in glacier melt, with big long grass coming up over our heads. That was probably the only time we felt in control: we reckoned we were quite hard core then, like we were in one of those action movies! We eventually rose up out of the river and ran over these huge sand dunes for about twenty miles. There were times we thought we wouldn't finish the race and when we did finally cross the finish line I felt humbled because I felt I hadn't beaten the conditions or the terrain; I'd barely passed the test. Forty-two people started the race, six dropped out and some got a lift part of the way, and we came joint 25th place. We were pleased with that, especially considering we had been second last at the end of the first day.

'During those first three days I thought it was the worst decision of my life to do the race, but looking back now I realise it's probably one of the best things I've ever done. And it will probably remain one of the best things I've done for a whole range of reasons, some very selfish, because the challenge right at the start was effectively a personal one: I basically wanted to run it to see if I could actually complete it. Although it started from personal reasons, at least I raised a reasonable amount of money for charity at the same time. €15,000 was donated to the Irish wing of Sight Savers International as a result of the race and €8,000 from my competing in the North Pole Marathon, although there is still money coming in for that. The reason I chose Sight Savers as opposed to the Irish Guide Dogs for the Blind or the National Council for the Blind of Ireland was because, in many respects, I feel privileged to be a blind person in Ireland as opposed to being blind in Africa or India. I've got my computer, which talks back to me, and there was never any question that I wouldn't get all the operations to make sure that if there was any possibility of me seeing that I would be able to see now. Cataract operations are routine here, not like in developing countries where Sight Savers operates. For €30 Sight Savers can change someone's life by literally making them see.'

Understandably, Mark felt his world had caved in the day he lost his sight. He was just weeks away from sitting his final exams at Trinity College Dublin and he had a 'fantastic' job offer in London. But that all changed overnight. 'I didn't think I was going to get my degree and I thought I'd never work, I'd never row again and I would never meet any girls,' he says. 'I felt my life was over. One week I was about to get my degree, the next I wasn't sitting my finals and I couldn't go to London. I couldn't even tell the time or walk outside the house by myself. I didn't just lose my sight that day; I lost my identity as well. Everything I was doing wasn't me any more; it was sort of a new version of me. I had been very independent, but suddenly I was reliant on other people for everything. All my norms were gone.'

Based on the work he had already completed Mark was, in fact, awarded a degree by Trinity. He soon got himself a white cane and a guide dog and then enrolled on a computer course to learn how to use speech software. Within months he was back in Dublin, living independently. He spent eighteen months working in the head office of the Irish Agricultural Wholesale Society, before moving to a management consultancy, but it was not until he started rowing again that he really felt his life was coming together. 'I was competing with the guys I used to compete with and going to the pub with the guys I used to hang around with,' he says. 'I was having the same kind of fun again and I began to feel more positive.'

In 2002 the management consultancy 'went bust', but Mark went on to complete a Master's at the Smurfit Business School. He is now based in Trinity where he is undertaking post-doctoral research into strategies for individual and team success. As if that wasn't enough, he has also become highly sought after for his inspiring presentations on motivation and is writing a book on the power of effective decision-making. Not only has he forged a new identity for himself, but he has also come to view his blindness as 'an inconvenience rather than a life-stopping disability'. He says, 'I never wake up thinking, "O no, I can't see!" although I do accept now that there are some things I cannot do. However, all the big things in my world: work, study, sport, girls, all of those things are fine. My life is probably different than what I would have done when I could see, but I'm still doing many of the same things.'

Mark is certainly living out his belief that 'the impossible is too often the untried' and it is thanks to both his and Richard's determination to achieve what has never been attempted before that three Irish charities now have substantially more money in their coffers. Mark became the first blind man to run either the Gobi March or the North Pole Marathon. He is currently training for two events in which he hopes to compete in 2005 – a 24-hour kayaking event and an ironman triathlon, which will involve a two and a half mile swim, a 112-mile cycle and a marathon run. And on top of his phenomenal string of achievements in 2002, Richard took to the treadmill in 2003 to create three new world records. In the window of the Cuba bar, where the citizens of Galway could watch him, he became the fastest person to run 100 km (9 hours 25 minutes and 37 seconds) and the fastest person to run 100 miles (17 hours 46 minutes and 6 seconds) on a treadmill. He also set a record for the greatest distance covered within forty-eight hours, 150.6 miles, which he completed in twenty-seven hours!

Jonathan Irwin and Mary-Ann O'Brien

who set up
The Jack and Jill
Children's Foundation
in memory of their baby son Jack

Jonathan Irwin and Mary-Ann O'Brien breathed a sigh of relief when baby Jack arrived safely on 29 February 1996: a baby brother for six-year-old Lily and two-year-old Phonsie, whose twin had sadly been stillborn. 'Jack was perfect – he weighed in at twelve pounds and he was absolutely fine,' remembers Jonathan. 'He was fabulously healthy,' adds Mary-Ann.

The following day, however, while Jack was in the nursery, medical staff rushed in to tell the proud new parents that they had just resuscitated Jack; he had suffered a near-miss cot death. 'Next time we saw him what we saw was not a healthy baby, but a little baby in an incubator with tubes all over the place,' says Jonathan. 'We knew he'd hit the end of the railway platform, as it were, and we really thought he wouldn't survive.'

After Jack had spent six weeks in intensive care, Jonathan and Mary-Ann asked to see the senior paediatrician. They were shocked by his brutal words. 'He told us, "You've got to understand that this is worse than just a tragedy" – that little Jack would, inadvertently, hinder the childhood of his healthy siblings and probably break up our marriage,' says Jonathan. 'I said we could take that on board and asked him for a route map. He replied, "Jonathan, I can tell you that in the Republic of Ireland in 1996 there is no route map." He pointed to Jack – who was blind and deaf and couldn't swallow – and said, "Jack is your only route map. My advice is to tell you to go home, pack a bag and bring Jack to one of the children's hospitals and get him admitted, knowing that you're going to abandon him. Then – and only then – will the State step forward and provide any assistance." It was terrible what he was saying; it made the hair stand up on the back of my head.'

Jonathan and Mary-Ann were 'absolutely stunned' to hear that the only solution to their predicament was to abandon their new born son; they could not possibly contemplate such a course of action. And so they returned home, determined to look after Jack as best they could. This was no easy task – he cried constantly and needed postural draining every hour as well as regular suctioning and physiotherapy. Their GP said he was not qualified to look after such a fragile little boy and if there were any emergencies they should drive straight to Crumlin Children's Hospital (this was not very reassuring, given that they live forty miles from Dublin in Ballitore, Co. Kildare). The local public health nurse called in once a week, but she could do little more than weigh the baby. 'She was a lovely lady and she'd come in for half an hour every Monday morning, but that left twenty-three and a half hours in that day and there were six other days of the week, each day an Everest,' says Jonathan.

'Jack was in a lot of distress and he cried twenty-four hours a day. The only way to feed him was through a nasal tube and, you know, it's not something that's very easy to do, especially when it comes out at four o'clock in the morning and you're exhausted and wondering if the tube's going into the lung rather than the tummy. The hospital called us once – not to see if we were coping with the tube or anything like that – but to ask when we were going to return their wind-up swing chair (at that stage it was our only way of getting Jack to sleep).'

'It was a total nightmare because he needed constant care and attention,' remembers Mary-Ann. 'We were constantly in and out of hospital and when we were at home it took up to eighteen hours a day to feed him. Can you imagine sticking a tube down someone's nose, especially when it's your own child and he's obviously not enjoying it? I can't imagine now how I ever did it. There were really bad days and sometimes Jack got epileptic fits. The only place he was ever really peaceful was in the bath – he loved being in the water because he completely relaxed and all his spasms went away. And so he spent up to five or six hours a day in the bath.'

Jonathan and Mary-Ann managed as best they could, but within three months they felt 'totally and absolutely flattened'. Neither was in a position to give up work – Jonathan headed up the Dublin Sports Council at that time and there was no way Mary-Ann was going to close the factory gates of her successful business, Lily O'Brien Chocolates, which she had set up four years earlier. One day one of the ladies who worked on the Lily O'Brien packing line, Nora Byrne, came up to Mary-Ann and said, 'Look, I've heard about your distress; I was a nurse before I was married and I'd love to meet Jack to see if I could get on with him.'

Nora was 'a natural' with him and over the next few months a few housewives in the area offered their services and soon Jack had a coterie of women caring for him around the clock. And so he was 'beautifully looked after' for the next eighteen months – until the day his tiny little heart gave up from the effort of trying to stay alive. 'He was a beautiful little boy and they all fell in love with him,' says Mary-Ann. 'They were incredibly positive, good people and having them around meant we suddenly felt we weren't on our own anymore. I felt much better – I stopped feeling utterly useless and crying all the time – and, by the time Jack died, it was like he had five mothers, not just me.'

The nursing rota 'worked so well' that Jonathan and Mary-Ann found it transformed their home from being a 'disastrously, desperately unhappy' one into an 'incredibly happy' one. And one evening, when Jack was a year old, they sat down at their kitchen table and decided they would have to 'do something' to help other people in similar situations. 'Unless you have outside help you just spend your whole day trying to stay alive and trying to keep your child alive,' says Mary-Ann. 'When you're in that situation any human who comes along and is willing to give you time and talk to you is a real godsend. There was absolutely nothing when Jack was born and we would have loved to have had some light in the tunnel.'

Having sat down, soon after Jack's birth, and rang every single children's charity listed in the Golden Pages, Jonathan knew there was no organisation that provided respite care for parents of severely brain-damaged children. There were day care centres in Dublin, but these were not available for people who lived 'down the country'. Jonathan commissioned the graduate school at University College Dublin to research the situation in Ireland and he found it was even worse than he had imagined. He says, 'It turned out, first of all, that there was no database to tell you how many Jack and Jill (in the good old days I would have said "severely handicapped") babies there were, which I find amazing. These babies are the most frail: they will never make the Special Olympics team, they'll never even practise for it. And so Mary-Ann and I determined that we would try and make certain that no other family would ever have to go through what we had been through. One way or another, we were going to find these babies all over Ireland and we were going to provide early intervention home respite. I interviewed a quite remarkable woman – Mary Joe Guilfoyle, who was very high up in Temple Street Hospital – and she bravely left her top position to start work with us in 1997. I was very impressed and very grateful because we didn't have any money in the bank at that stage.

'We then started fundraising and because I had worked in the horse industry – I ran Goff's and the Phoenix Park Racecourse – I was able to call in a lot of favours from the thirty-five years I had moved in that group. I got together a very healthy nest egg through a combination of people's generosity and various events. We had one unbelievable evening when I invited thirty-two prominent businessmen to a private function in a Dublin restaurant and the guest speaker was Vinnie Jones. It was phenomenal: he spoke so brilliantly and judged the rhythm of the room so well that we raised IR£750,000 that evening. It really gave me the oxygen to charge on.'

Seven years on The Jack and Jill Children's Foundation employs six paediatric nurses as well as four administrative staff. Despite the huge amount of time, effort and energy Jonathan has put into the organisation it was not until 2003 that he started to draw a salary for his work. Up until then all his efforts had been purely voluntary, as had Mary-Ann's, although her time was more limited as Lily O'Brien's had rapidly expanded in the same period (the total number of employees at her Newbridge factory had increased from forty to over one hundred). While it has been primarily Mary-Ann's role to 'earn the bread', many of her evenings continue to be taken up with Jack and Jill activities; she is responsible for the budget and organises the annual golf classic as well as giving regular talks and media interviews.

Before the Foundation came into being there was no group in the country helping the families of children under four who were born with or who had developed brain damage and suffered severe intellectual and physical developmental delay as a result. The organisation grew out of the shocking reality that services for these children and their families were not just underdeveloped, but, to all intents and purposes, were non-existent. Most people are unaware of this distressing 'age gap' in the healthcare services; Jonathan describes these babies and their parents as 'the forgotten people of Irish society'.

There are now about two hundred and thirty families on Jack and Jill's books. 'A child is usually referred to us by the maternity hospital or children's hospital and our liaison nurse for that area visits the family as soon as possible and she will talk to the GP and consultant,' says Jonathan. 'She then sends us a file and, together with the family, we devise a programme to best suit their needs. In some cases this will involve getting a nurse in three or four nights a week or, in less severe cases, it might just involve getting a mum-in-law to come in two hours a day so that mum can get out to the shops or spend time with her other children.

The money we give the families is a donation towards the wages of the nurses, the mother-in-law or friend for giving up those hours. What we're really doing is empowering the families to buy the services that they feel are most beneficial for their child.'

In the space of a few years Jonathan and Mary-Ann have managed to put together exactly the kind of organisation they wish had existed when Jack was born. 'It's great that people now have something to turn to,' says Mary-Ann. 'It's not that we're that great, it's just that there was nothing there before. If only we'd had a route map – like Jack and Jill gives people now – a support team, somebody to talk to and to have been put in touch with families who had similar experiences; it would have made such a difference. But there was nothing – absolutely nothing. Those first few months the marriage nearly went out the door; I had other children to think of, but I couldn't take them anywhere and there was never any question of having a family meal together. I can't describe the difference between looking after a normal child and one who should really be in an intensive care situation. And I know children are hard enough work when they're healthy! I don't know if we would have continued to cope if Nora Byrne hadn't come along; I'd say we couldn't have. And that's why we decided to do something like this for other people.'

The Jack and Jill Children's Foundation currently receives an annual grant of €317,000 from the government, but that is only a fraction of the amount of funding the organisation needs in order to function. Jonathan had to raise €1.6m in 2004 in order to continue the work. He is always on the lookout for new ways of fundraising and he particularly delights in finding methods that do not hurt the donor. 'I love mouse traps that save the donor money and which provide money for the charity at the same time,' he says. 'We've started a scheme with the telecom company, Greencom, whereby if you sign up with them ten per cent of every call you make goes directly to Jack and Jill. It just shows what margins the telecom companies are making because not only do we have the potential of unbelievable earnings, but people's telephone bills go down quite amazingly. I like the idea of philanthropic giving that doesn't hurt anybody. The other absolutely brilliant idea, which came from the recycling company Folamh, was a scheme for recycling printer cartridges. Only five per cent of used inkjet, laser and fax toner cartridges are currently recycled in Ireland and yet by simply sticking them in a special envelope and posting them to Folamh they're worth €2.50 per cartridge to us. I think turning waste material into money for charity is brilliant!'

Jonathan is delighted that many Jack and Jill families take it upon themselves to organise fundraising efforts: in the past eighteen months they have raised over €250,000. As well as fundraising, Jonathan has also become an advocate for the families involved. He was shocked to discover, following Jack's birth, that although his son was eligible for a Domiciliary Care Allowance, he would not receive it until he turned two. After considerable lobbying Jonathan managed to get this situation changed. 'You have very little idea how unkind the offices of the State are to families,' he says. 'And it's not just about money; it's about caring for people. When Jack was born nobody told us what we were entitled to, which was very frustrating. Now we are in a position to advise families. I have found that the more humble a person's circumstances the more unkind the State is: you're really made to get down and grovel to get what your child is entitled to. I do find that TDs and ministers are accessible, though, and they are alert to trying to help; it's quite extraordinary how the health board offices crumble in the face of an active TD. I cannot understand why Jack and Jill babies do not qualify for a medical card until they turn sixteen and I think I will be forced to take action against the State on behalf of, say, three nominated families and their children. We can never make Jack and Jill babies better, but we can try and make the family's lives a little easier.'

Fionnuala and Jonathan Brocklebank were told about The Jack and Jill Children's Foundation when their three-week-old son, Robert, suffered profound brain damage following a bout of ecoli septiceamia with secondary meningitis. He immediately lost all control of his head and trunk and within six months he lost the swallowing reflex. Not wishing to consider themselves 'a charity case' the Brocklebanks decided against contacting the organisation, but after five months of being confined to the house twenty-four hours a day Fionnuala finally contacted Jonathan Irwin. Looking back now, she is so grateful she took that step and she cannot imagine how she would have coped if the Foundation had not been there to provide her with the kind of help she needed.

'It doesn't really bear thinking about,' says Fionnuala. 'Robert was tube-fed from seven months and I couldn't leave him in the care of anyone other than a nurse because he had to be constantly monitored for convulsions. He cried for hours and hours and hours – a very distressed, high-pitched cry – and he had uncontrollable muscle spasms, which could be minimised (to a certain extent) through handling. Sometimes I walked the floor with him all day and all night.

'I had to give up work, which meant Jonathan had to work extra hours to make up the shortfall. There was no way we could have afforded to pay for any kind of help; you'd have to have mega bucks to afford any kind of care. Jack and Jill gave us IR£800 a month – that equated to ten hours per night for eight nights in the month. It takes a lot of the pressure off if you know that two times a week you are going to get a proper night's sleep because you have a nurse whom you trust wholeheartedly with your child. The Jack and Jill liaison nurse, Mags, was always available to talk to; she offered practical advice, made us aware of our entitlements and, if necessary, we knew she would liaise with the local health service.

'Nothing could possibly prepare you for something like that happening in your life and there will never be words to describe how you could be so delighted about someone coming to the door and helping you. It's a terrible predicament to be in and when your situation is so desperate any small bit of help or act of kindness is appreciated so much. I'll never forget one Easter when Robert was in hospital and Mags came in with two Lily O'Brien Easter eggs – it was a lovely gesture.

'We knew Robert probably wouldn't reach his second birthday and, after months and months of being in chronic distress, he died at twenty-two months. He gradually went into multi-organ failure and, by the time of his death, he was basically unrecognisable as Robert – as the beautiful baby he was when he was younger. After he died Jonathan wrote to us personally – stating that Robert had been an icon and a champion of everything The Jack and Jill Children's Foundation strived to achieve. I thought that was so lovely. He is a wonderful, wonderful man and I can't thank him enough.'

Helen and Stephen Ward were told about The Jack and Jill Children's Foundation after their son's birth in 1999. Due to a lack of oxygen, baby Jack's brain had completely shrivelled, leaving him blind, epileptic and with cerebral palsy. Now aged four, he has the mental age of a three or four month old baby. Initially his parents were told he would have to be tube-fed and that he would have to stay in hospital for the first eight weeks of his life. But when he was two weeks old a nurse tried him with a bottle and, much to his parents' delight, he took an ounce. They started bottle-feeding him themselves and a few days later they were allowed to take him home. Before they left hospital a social worker asked them if they would like The Jack and Jill Children's Foundation to contact them; they said yes, although they had no idea what to expect from the organisation.

'When we brought Jack home from hospital we were feeling completely dazed,' says Helen. 'We got a phone call from The Jack and Jill Children's Foundation that day and a liaison nurse came out to us the following day. To be honest, we didn't know what to expect from them, but they were unbelievable. The nurses are special people and I can't praise Jonathan and Mary-Ann enough either: to go through what they went through and to think, "Right, we'll help other families now." Most people would just feel sorry for themselves and that would be that.

'For the first eight months Jack just cried and cried and cried; it was a very high pitched cry. I know now that that's very common with children like that. Stephen used to say to him, "Where's your instruction book? We've fed you, winded you and changed you." We just didn't know what to do for him and we felt absolutely devastated. A number of my friends and neighbours had babies around the same time and I felt very much, "Why me?" Not that I begrudged them their healthy babies or anything like that, but I couldn't help wondering why it had happened to poor Jack. I just felt he had never done anything to anybody to deserve this. The anger I felt was absolutely unbelievable.'

Jack's incessant crying eased off when he reached eight months and it was around this time Helen and Stephen learned that he was epileptic (he was having up to 150 seizures every day) and blind. Well, he can see all right – his optic nerve is fine – but his damaged brain cannot make any sense of the information it receives. So to all intents and purposes, Jack might as well be blind and has been registered as such. At eleven months he began to attend St Joseph's School for the Blind in Drumcondra one day a week; he now goes four days a week. Whereas he used to hate the noise of other children, he now loves to hear them and he has become much more sociable.

'Jack's normally very happy these days,' says Helen. 'If you see tears it means there's something wrong; he doesn't cry for no reason anymore. We're very, very lucky with him; there's a lot of children, like Jack, who suffer from chest infections constantly, whereas Jack has only ever had one. He doesn't have to be tube-fed: he eats puréed food and high calorie supplement drinks. But his only way of communicating is a high-pitched shriek and I haven't a clue what he's trying to say. The speech therapists and neurologist doubt very much that he'll develop speech because he hasn't even got to the baby stage of gurgling. They told me to mimic him. If I shriek he smiles, but the neighbours must think I'm mad!

'He can't walk and he doesn't use his hands for anything; if you put a toy in his hand it's like he doesn't even realise it's there. We got a dog to see if that would help: if you take his hand he'll open it to stroke the dog, but normally his hand is clenched with the thumb inside the fingers. I'm doing a Brainwave physiotherapy programme with him twice a day in the hopes that one day I'll get him to use his hands because if you put him in a chair and he starts to slide he doesn't put his arms out to stop himself from sliding. All I'd really like for him to do is to be able to sit up by himself. In the beginning I hoped he'd see, I hoped he'd walk, I hoped he'd talk, but I think I'm beginning to get a bit more real now. If he could only sit up by himself I'd be happy.

'In the early days I was always asking "Why me?" but I'm much better now. I still have bad days when I have to pull the blind down on the window because I can't bear to see kids the same age as Jack – and younger – out playing on the road. I feel he should be out there, too. People say to me that he doesn't know any better, but I do; I know he should be out there playing. I used to have more bad days than good, but I knew the Jack and Jill nurses were always at the end of the phone. If I was having a really bad day, the liaison nurse would be the first person I'd ring: she could listen to me for an hour crying down the phone and she'd never complain. When I was refused a carer's allowance she was the first person I rang. She told me how to appeal the decision and I managed to get it in the end. Jonathan has been fantastic, too: I remember ranting and raving at him about the fact we're entitled to a petrol allowance from the health board, but not until you've purchased a specially adapted car (to accommodate a wheelchair). He calmed me down and explained the ins and outs and how much they've been campaigning about that issue.

'It's nice to know there's someone always watching your back, looking out for you and trying to do the best for your child. Also, through Jack and Jill we've learned that we're not the only ones with a brain-damaged child and that there are people worse off than us. At least we have Jack – he's alive, he's at home and he doesn't have to be tube-fed. So we realise there's a lot of pluses for us.'

Helen and Stephen are relieved that their son does not need nursing care and they use their monthly Jack and Jill allowance to get out for an evening every week. They don't use teenage babysitters, but trusted friends and neighbours who have known Jack since he was born. 'We have a huge circle of friends and there's usually something happening at the weekend,' says Helen. 'If not, then myself and Stephen can get out together – just the two of us – which is brilliant. We'd be lost without the allowance; I can't imagine what it would be like because our families don't live nearby. In fact, if it wasn't for Jack and Jill I think I'd have gone off my head altogether. I couldn't go back to work because we couldn't find a creche that was willing to take a child with epilepsy; a seizure could take Jack at any time and no creche wants that responsibility.

'I just can't find the words to say how grateful I am to Jack and Jill, or how much I admire Jonathan, Mary-Ann and the nurses. They definitely are special people. A lot of Jack and Jill babies have died and they would have been attached to them – how they do it I don't know. I think they're special angels; that's the only way I can describe them. We would have been lost without them and we try to do some fundraising to give a little back: I organise a fashion show every year and this year I ran the mini-marathon. Stephen has done a head shave and he organised a golf classic. So we do bits and pieces and it gives me something to think about other than appointments and medicine. We could never pay them back, however; if I gave them €10m it wouldn't pay them back for everything they've done for us in the past four years.'

Jonathan Irwin is constantly 'on the road' receiving cheques and thanking people for their fundraising efforts as well as giving talks to various groups. He was delighted when The Jack and Jill Children's Foundation received the Children of Ireland Award 2003. 'I was delighted for the nurses, I really was,' he says. 'And it was fabulous publicity for a young charity - a stamp of approval that we're really doing something useful.'

Mary-Ann reckons her husband is 'in love' with his charity work. 'He never says no to anybody,' she says. 'He's a fantastic speaker and he's very good at galvanising a roomful of people towards him. He'll be off to a fashion show in Waterford one week and he'll be having dinner with two hundred ladies in Galway the next. There's no doubt but Jack and Jill is extremely fulfilling and, hopefully, one day I too will go on to have much more involvement.

'The little boy Jack was a mighty person when you look at what he created (I'll never do anything as much in all my lifetime) and he was only alive for eighteen months! It's very nice to be the Mummy of someone who's done such a great job. So, basically it's a very happy ending. Even though I was hysterical when Jack died, at the end of the day it's cruel to keep someone like that alive; he had no quality of life whatsoever. We thought he would survive forever – we'd even built a wheelchair accessible extension onto our house – but I'm glad that he didn't. I really am, because he's got to be better off where he is now.'

Beni Oburu, Assiomowu Olabisi Shittu, Omolabake Ayoade and Erica Birch-Abban

whose community work just goes to show how much immigrants and asylum seekers have to offer Irish society

Whatever way you look at it, Ireland simply is not the same as it used to be. Whereas twenty years ago anything other than a pasty white face was a rarity, now there are people of all races, colours and creeds to be found living in even the remotest corners of the island. Economic migrants and asylum seekers alike have brought with them diversity and vitality and very often these newcomers have sought to become involved in their local communities.

When Beni Oburu and her family arrived in rural north Cork in 1994, they were a huge novelty in the area and Beni was determined that they would settle in and feel at home. She found out about the local history and she enjoyed listening to local and national radio. She already knew a fair bit about Ireland because she was taught by Irish nuns in her native Kenya and she has always been grateful to the Irish for her education. When she turned eleven her parents could no longer afford to send her to school and if it wasn't for 'the pennies for the black baby' donated by people thousands of miles away she would not have been allowed stay on in school. In fact, so indebted did she feel that when she set foot on Irish soil several decades later the first person she looked up was Sr Mary Joseph, her favourite nun from schooldays.

When her youngest daughter, Ruth, started attending Adair National School in 1994 Beni had no intention of sitting around at home. She wanted to get involved in the community and so she asked if there was anything she could do to help in the school. 'I volunteered because I wanted to integrate and interact with the community, to learn their ways and I felt that the school was the heart of society,' says Beni. 'It was a two-teacher school and the teacher of the senior classes, Heather Smith, said she had chosen 'People' as her theme for the year and asked, seeing as we were the first black family in the area, if I would like to tell the pupils about where I came from. So I went in and told them about Kenya and about African people.'

The children loved listening to Beni's stories and learning the songs and dances that she herself had learned as a child; and her visits to the school soon became a regular feature. And so, just as Beni could name the thirty-two counties and sing 'It's a Long Way to Tipperary' as a child, so the local children were soon able to perform Kenyan dances and songs and speak a few words of Swahili. Soon she also had them making toys out of materials that would normally end up in the bin – they learned how to turn plastic bags into footballs and they wove sisal grass, a fibre which grows naturally in Kenya, into skipping ropes. They also learned how to weave grass skirts and to make percussion instruments out of baked bean tins filled with stones. 'One thing that struck me when I came to the western world (especially when I studied child care in England) was the amount of toys available for children – toys that challenge different parts of their growth. It made a lot of sense to me – that different toys challenged hand-eye co-ordination or fine or large motor skills and that the whole idea of these toys is so that a child can grow holistically to become a whole adult. But it made me think about the fact that we didn't have all these different toys in Africa. I didn't have any toys as a kid, except what I made, and yet I'd like to think that I'm as good as the person beside me. It got me thinking back to my own childhood – we didn't buy toys and we didn't have any in school, but we made them – and in the process of making them and playing with them we were developing the same kinds of skills. That sparked an interest in me and that's why I started showing the children in school how we would have made our own toys.'

Beni's activities with the children reminded Heather Smith of a seminar she had attended in Limerick University. A lecturer from Dublin had talked about bringing that kind of education to Ireland – an education to help Irish children to appreciate that children from other parts of the world may be poor or of another colour, but that they have the same basic needs. She looked up her notes and discovered that the lecturer was Bet Aalen, who lectures in Trinity College Dublin and in the Church of Ireland Teacher Training College. She got in touch with Bet and told her that Beni was doing exactly the kind of thing Bet said should be happening in schools. Bet was delighted to hear this and said she would like to come and visit. 'When we heard she was coming we decided to make a big thing out of it,' says Beni. 'We decided the children would put together a presentation, explaining about all the different activities and all that they had learnt. We had songs and dances and African food and we invited all the parents too. Unbeknown to us, Bet had been on sabbatical in Kenya and she came dressed in African clothes. I was amazed! Bet said that what I was doing was exactly the kind of thing she had been working towards and that she would look at ways we might be able to apply for funding from the Department of Foreign Affairs. She asked if I would like to visit other schools in the meantime. I said if it would benefit anybody, I'd be delighted to. After all, I received an education from Irish nuns and if I could give something back I'd be delighted.'

Bet arranged for Beni to visit schools all over Ireland, including Mullingar, Laois and Sligo. A Cultural Links committee was formed and in 1995 it was allocated £4000 to carry out a feasibility study, which turned out to be 'very positive'. They were then given a certain amount of funding, which has gradually increased over the years, so now Beni is able to continue doing the same kind of work that she did voluntarily for a number of years, but now she gets paid for it. 'For the first few years I was not working for money, but I was building up a reputation,' says Beni. 'Talking about volunteering, the committee members who help me do not accept any money. They were aware of my personal story – I have to send money back to my family in Kenya – and they were eager to help me become self-sufficient. I worked hard to get my work permit and they were willing to do whatever it took to help me; they totally and utterly refused payment.'

The Development Education Unit of the Department of Foreign Affairs has asked Beni to rewrite her programme to fit in with the curriculum. She is currently doing this as well as pursuing a two-year development studies' course at University College Cork. She has also been involved in putting together a gender, equality and multicultural video, which will be shown in schools throughout Ireland. She also helped draw up the cultural aspects of the new Social Personal Health Education programme. 'Every summer I give teachers in-service training and I also work with the Church of Ireland College of Education and Mary Immaculate College,' says Beni. 'I tried the new programme with them, but they preferred the old one because they felt it had more impact. The new programme teaches the same principles – of helping children in Ireland to appreciate that children in the developing world have the same needs as them (although these are met differently) – but it is done primarily through storytelling. The teachers felt anybody could come in and do what I'm doing now, but that it takes someone with a background like mine to do what I used to do. I do miss my old programme, to be honest. Like them, I felt that it made more of an impact.'

An important aspect of Beni's work is to challenge people's stereotypes. Under her old programme, the first thing she would do when she visited a new school was to hold up a picture of a beautiful modern city and ask pupils to guess where it was.

Invariably, ninety-nine per cent of them would guess New York. 'They were always amazed when I told them that it was Nairobi, the capital of Kenya,' says Beni. 'I'd say to them that sometimes we need to change our thinking about things and we'd talk about the different kinds of people we see in Ireland. I'd then show them pictures of shanty towns and we'd talk about poor children and about food, education and clean water. And we'd talk about how if a child's parents couldn't afford to buy him toys, then he had to make his own.'

Sometimes Beni would ask school children to write a poem about another culture. She has kept a collection of these and there is one, in particular, which she often quotes when she is addressing teachers' meetings. It is by Aaron Quinn, a former pupil of St Patrick's National School, Greystones. He wrote it when he was eleven.

Who Cares?

What's in a face?
Slanted eyes,
Afro hair,
Yellow skin,
Freckles.
Who cares?
It's what's in the heart that counts.

What's in a creed?
Skull caps,
The Bible,
Rosary beads,
The Koran.
Who cares?
It's what's in the heart that counts.

What's in a language?
Dia duit,
Guten tag,
Jambo,

Bonjour.
Who cares?
It's what's in the heart that counts.

What's in a home?
A thatched roof,
A block of flats,
Tin walls,
A cardboard box.
Who cares?
It's what's in the heart that counts.

Beni's volunteer work in schools may have transformed into full-time paid work, but she has not abandoned her volunteering spirit. She is a founding member of two local support groups for foreign nationals, Integrate Fermoy and Integrate Mallow, which focus on education and on raising awareness, as well as social activities. Unlike when they first arrived, Beni and her family are no longer the only black people in their area. There are now four Nigerian, two Ghanaian and two South African families. 'I feel more part of the community than they do,' says Beni. 'It's kind of interesting sometimes because when I'm with black people they will speak freely because I'm one of them, but I have been in a position in Ireland when there weren't many black people and we were accepted for who we were. We were not a threat to anybody – we were just us and we were accepted for that. We have the benefit of having seen Ireland where people were not wary of us, but now there's a bit of wariness because the numbers of black people have increased. I'm glad that people have not changed towards us because they knew us from before and we had already made a name for ourselves.'

When Assimowu Olabisi Shittu arrived in Dundalk in 2000 she was one of the first black people to live in the town, although there are now several hundred non-nationals living there. Like Beni, she too was something of a novelty. 'I think I came at the right time because everybody was really nice to me,' she says. 'People wanted to talk to me and I remember when I was walking down the street one day an old man stopped me and asked if he could touch me. He wasn't being rude; I think it was just that he'd never met a black person before. I never got any negative remarks from people, but when a lot of black people started coming to Dundalk then all this negative stuff started appearing in the newspapers.'

As soon as she arrived in Dundalk Assi, as she is known (it's easier for Irish people to get their tongue around), offered to help out in St Joseph's National School, where she had enrolled her daughter, Chioma. She became involved in the lunch club, making sandwiches every morning before school for any children who came to school without lunch. She also became involved in the homework club, helping children with their Maths and English and introducing them to craftwork from Africa and around the world. St Joseph's has a large number of international pupils, including children from Eastern Europe as well as Africa. 'The other parents who help out are all Irish, but because I've been involved a long time now I feel I belong there,' says Assi. 'I don't feel any different. Sometimes they say negative things about black people, but then they'd say, 'Oh, but Assi, you're not like that!' I just wanted to get involved because I think it's boring to sit and do nothing. I'm not a TV person; I like doing things.

'I did a diploma in special needs at the School of Practical Childcare in Dublin, which helps me with the homework club – not that there's anything wrong with the children, but some are just hyper! As an asylum seeker I can't do paid work, but if I could I would like to be a classroom assistant. Now I'm doing a four-year degree course in Borderland Studies in Dundalk Institute of Technology. It includes media, computers, culture, politics and archaeology – and I'm enjoying it because I now know more about Irish history and culture. I'm lucky I have a strong community around me; I think I'm blessed. I go to the pub with Irish friends, sometimes with African friends too. You don't have to be drinking to go to the pub. In Africa women belong to the house; I'd never been in a pub before I came to Ireland!'

It was only a matter of time before Assi was invited to give talks to teachers and parents on issues relating to life as an asylum seeker and on other intercultural matters. She then found herself in the classroom, doing a similar kind of volunteer work as Beni. She is now hugely committed to this kind of educational work and has a deep appreciation for the need to build intercultural understanding through interaction, information and sharing experiences.

In 2001 Assi became a founding member of the Louth African Women's Support Group, which visits different schools in Co Louth to present cultural awareness days. 'I thought we needed something because there were so many bad things being said about Africans as a result of misunderstandings,' she says. 'My Irish friends were telling me that when they said hello to an African on the street the African would not look at them. I explained it's not that they're being rude, but that it's part of our culture: it's a form of disrespect to look at someone straight in the eyes, especially if they are older. Teachers, too, were baffled as to why children wouldn't look them in the eyes; they thought the kids were hiding something from them. When I came to Ireland I had to learn to look in people's eyes; I'm well able to do it now. And so I felt Africans needed a voice, that we needed to stand up for ourselves, and that we needed to do it before it was too late. If not for ourselves, then at least for the sake of our children.'

'We go into schools dressed in our cultural dress and we talk to the children; we bring in African food and pictures of Africa and we ask if they have any questions. They usually ask us what the weather is like in Africa. When we went to the Dundalk Institute of Technology someone asked if we get free cars! People can't understand how we can afford cars; they have this idea that we're given them and that social welfare pays our insurance. We let them know that that is not the way it is. I asked the students how much they spent in the pub each week. Some said €50, others said as much as €100. So I said, "Look, this is it. I don't drink and I don't smoke because it's not part of my culture. Everybody has their own priorities. We do our shopping in bulk, we go to the supermarket once every two weeks, and we do all our own cooking; we never eat out. That's where the difference is."'

Assi is in no doubt that talking to young people in the area is helping to promote understanding between cultures. 'It definitely makes a difference,' she says. 'I did one talk with some early school leavers – I don't want to call them drop outs, but they're very negative kids and the woman who runs the group told me to be ready for anything. By the time I'd finished talking to them it was fine and now when they see me on the street they always say hello to me. And that's good. I know we can't catch everybody, but at least we can catch a few people on our side who think, "Look, they're not what people think they are."

Since her arrival in Dundalk, Assi has also been involved in One World Spirit where she volunteers as an information officer one day a week, offering support, encouragement and guidance to other asylum seekers. 'Sometimes people will come with a social welfare problem, but you don't have to have a problem to come to the clinic; some of them live in the hostel and it's good for them just to come down and have a cup of tea. Some people need assistance with medical appointments because the language barrier can give problems. I speak French and English and sometimes I accompany people to their medical appointments to help them communicate with the doctors. I just try to do what I can.'

Assi also responds to requests from service providers – social workers, midwives and youth workers – for information sessions on cultural awareness. 'Some of the nurses and midwives don't understand why so many people will come into hospital and visit an African woman after she has given birth. I explain to them that it is simply part of our culture; even though you know the mother's coming home soon you still want to visit in hospital.'

She is also a regional representative for Integration Ireland, an umbrella group for different organisations dealing with immigrants and asylum seekers, and she is a board member of Dundalk's Women's Awareness Group. She is also on the management committee of a Community Parenting Support Programme. 'The Community Mothers visit African mothers, but they don't know how to support them,' says Assi. 'I have hosted training sessions for them, advising them on how to approach young African mothers. I tell them not to ask too many questions when they visit the first time because African mothers don't know where they're coming from. They might not understand that they're coming to support them; some of them will still have asylum cases waiting and they might not understand that this is a support scheme, completely separate from the Department of Justice, and so they may be afraid. They need to ask about the kids first; that's how they can build a relationship with them. If they ask too many questions, the next time they go the African mother will not open her door to them. I do not visit mothers, unless they request to see an African. One woman had bad depression after her baby was born and her child was taken away from her. I went to see the woman and eventually she got her child back. I became so close to another woman I visited that I became the godmother of her son.'

Assi herself is an asylum seeker, still awaiting permission to remain in the country. Understandably, it's a nerve-racking time for her. Her spirits were lifted, however, when she received a World Refugee Day Award in June 2003 in the 'education and youth' category. She was nominated by the chairperson of One World Spirit, Colette O'Regan, with the backing of people from the many different organisations Assi has devoted herself to in the few years since she arrived in Ireland. 'I was really shocked to receive the award,' says Assi. 'I mean you just do these things and you don't really think about it. I was really, really delighted, though, that at least people were seeing the good part of me. It's good that there's many people working hard, giving their time to improve things for refugees in Ireland – not only African people, but Irish people too.

'The one shock I did get recently was the result of the referendum on 11 June. To be honest, I was expecting the Yes vote to win, but the depressing, shocking news was when I saw it was nearly eighty per cent. That gave me a bit of a shock. And it was even more of a shock to see that my county was the third highest Yes vote in the whole country. But I don't want to look at it as a negative Yes; we have to consult ourselves and say, "This is not about racism; it's about what people want." It's hard to know, but maybe it was out of a fear of the unknown. Perhaps people felt, "We have to stop this; this is a small place, not like America." I just keep hoping that people will understand that although we have our bad eggs, Africans are not all bad. It's just because we're new and people have this fear; they don't know where all these people are coming from and it's not easy for them to trust us. I feel the intercultural awareness projects I'm involved in are helping to make a difference, even though they won't change the whole of Ireland.'

Like Assi and Beni, Omolabake Ayoade became involved in various community programmes when she arrived in Ireland from her native Nigeria five years ago. She attended various courses and soon found herself giving cultural awareness talks to parents, teachers, pupils and different organisations. 'We let people know what it's like to experience a racist attack and we discuss with teachers if children of foreign nationals have some kind of behaviour that they might not understand,' says Omolabake. 'Our backgrounds are different from Irish people's backgrounds, so we discuss some issues.'

It was on one of these courses that Omolabake met Florence Burns, who is a family development nurse overseeing the Community Mothers Programme in part of Tallaght. Omolabake, who has two young sons, volunteered to become a Community Mother and, after completing four training sessions, she started to visit local mothers, mostly other foreign nationals living in her locality. 'I have visited one Irish family, but otherwise the families I have visited have been from Poland, Romania, Sri Lanka and different African countries,' she says. 'The first family I visited was from India, but it turned out they had spent some time living in Nigeria. So I've met a lot of people from different cultures and I've learnt from them and also they've learnt from me because we have shared our experiences. I am very glad that I am able to empathise with people and to make a difference in people's lives. That makes me very, very happy.

'The programme helps so many people, especially foreign nationals who don't have anybody here. Back home they would have the support of family and friends, but here they're on their own. In my own country if somebody has a child, for the next forty-one days the woman will not do anything: she will just wake up, bath and feed the baby because her mother or mother-in-law will be there to help her. But coming here is so different because there's nobody. Some women cry from morning to night; some don't have any experience and they start crying when their baby cries. I think it's good the African mothers have the support of someone from their own culture because it gives them more confidence.

'One woman was having difficulties breastfeeding and the baby kept crying. I wanted to encourage her to breastfeed and I gave her information that helped her overcome the problems. I was so happy then when she continued breastfeeding for the next few months. I did research into breastfeeding when I was doing a pre-nursing course in Inchicore College and so I like to tell people the advantages of breastfeeding because some people don't know. With the training I have had and with my own experience I share with the mothers and boost their self-esteem. I give them encouragement and let them know that they are important to their children. Even if nobody thanks you for the job you do, you should know that you are doing a great job because if you bring your children up properly they are the future and they will be useful to the community.

'We give the mothers information on diet, health, child development and language. Some people don't realise that at six months it's a good idea to start reading to your baby. So there is fun, support and information and generally they are very happy with the programme: it is very, very interesting and so many people have benefited from it. Most families continue for about a year and I do an evaluation with them and from their comments I realise they really, really appreciate it. And they really enjoy it. I think the programme helps prevent depression because it relieves stress from people; some mothers are tensed up when they have problems with their child and they've nobody to turn to. Talking eases their stress. We don't give any medical advice, but we advise them to talk to their GP or the public health nurse if there are any health worries. If there's a child who I think needs to be weighed or has a little problem I can talk to Florence and she will talk to the public health nurse, who may go to visit the child.'

Approximately one thousand families in Dublin receive monthly visits from Community Mothers at any one time, mostly in disadvantaged areas. Florence says the scheme enhances the work of the public health nurse rather than replacing it. 'We believe that the parents are the experts on their own child and we hope to empower parents in their parenting role by providing information on child development relevant to the age of their baby,' says Florence. 'Oftentimes it's just encouragement that's needed because they're doing a fine job anyway. The programme is for regular families, not for families in distress, but it is to prevent distress happening. We hope that by giving information mothers will be further motivated. I love having the multicultural dimension and even though families have different ways of doing things, the areas that we're working on, like talking to your baby and reading to him, covers every culture. Whether people's daily staple is yams or spuds is irrelevant because we're not telling them they have to become like the Irish.'

Omolabake is waiting to see if she will be granted asylum to stay in Ireland. If she is, she would love to work as a nurse's aide. Meanwhile, she is heavily involved with Tallaght Intercultural Action – a group of foreign nationals from various countries who have done many different courses, including one with Travellers. 'I've done lots of courses learning about other people's cultures,' she says. 'I think when you learn about different people's cultures you learn that it's not good to generalise about people. Doing all those courses with different groups I've learned so much; it's good to diversify and it's good to mix with people.'

Erica Birch-Abban, who went to live in Letterkenny when she arrived in Ireland from her native Ghana in 2003, has been involved in various courses at the local women's centre. She has also attended gender equality conferences and she has found that Irish people are often interested to learn more about African culture. 'Culturally we have to adapt to the Irish way of doing things,' says Erica. 'There's this saying, "When in Rome do as the Romans do," so we do what the Romans do. But we also want the Romans to know at least a little about us, so that when they see us doing something they're not used to they will understand we do these things because it is our culture, and so they will accept us the way we are.

'The other day I was talking to a mechanic and when he told me his price I tried to bargain with him because we bargain in Africa. It's an in-built thing, something we grew up with, so anywhere we go we try to bargain. The mechanic was so mad at me and I asked him why he was so angry (I didn't think I'd done anything to offend him). He said, 'Yeah, you did because you tried to bargain.' He said he wasn't doing an auction! The next time I went to see him I didn't try to bargain and he was so calm and nice; it was a total transformation. I told him I'd understood why he'd got angry, but that I wanted him to understand that it is something Africans are used to; anything we buy, we bargain. So really I hadn't intended to offend him; bargaining was just something that came naturally to me. He said he understood.'

Erica finds it frustrating that as an asylum seeker she is not allowed to do paid work. In Ghana she worked as a personnel officer for an Australian company, but her heart was in the voluntary work she did as a radio presenter with Twin City FM. 'It was something I loved to do,' she says. 'I did three shows, a talk show in the morning, a lunchtime special of soft music for relaxation and a 'midnight groove' show, which was also soft music. I did it for about three years and it's something I wanted to do again. I hope to make a full-time career of radio presentation some day.'

When Erica arrived in Letterkenny she soon discovered that the local station, Highland Radio, did not have any shows featuring African culture or music, even though there are about five hundred Africans living in Co. Donegal. She rang the station and proposed an African-flavoured show and the management said they would get back to her. The result? Erica now hosts a half-hour show once a month called *The Voice of Africa*. On the first show she interviewed an Irish lady who had spent three years doing voluntary work in Kenya and who now works with Africans in Donegal. Since then her guests have included a

Nigerian lady who spoke about Nigerian culture and the local youth information officer, who is currently spearheading an intercultural project. The shows also features African music. 'The programme is all about Africa and interculturalism,' says Erica. 'I think that's very important because we cannot live hand-in-hand with each other and peacefully if we don't know about each other's cultures. I've had a good response from people so far. During the show people ring in and make comments about how they love the music and how they love the show. Interestingly enough, all the calls are from Irish people. The show is really aimed at Irish people because I realised there were too many stereotypes concerning Africans, especially asylum seekers. That's why it has been my intention to invite people in to talk about their cultures and at least try to break some of the stereotypes.'

Erica was also involved in founding the Donegal African Women's Association, which came up with the novel idea of holding an African fashion show to raise money for People in Need. This took place in May 2004 in conjunction with the Donegal Women's Network and the Second Chance Education Project for Women. 'I was MC for the evening and I explained about the different outfits,' says Erica. 'Everybody was very impressed by the colours and everything; they said they'd never seen anything like it. We raised over €1000 for People in Need.

'In general I find Irish people very friendly and hospitable. I will never forget a nurse I met on the maternity ward at Letterkenny Hospital when I first came to Donegal. I was very frustrated because I didn't know anybody, I was ill and pregnant and I had my two young children with me. I went to the hospital and because it was the weekend the community welfare officer wasn't working. This nurse organised temporary accommodation for me and, as I was leaving, she said, "Take this", and put something in my hand. It was €60! And this was somebody I didn't know! She was so, so good to me and I will never forget her.

'Sometimes I do find the attitudes of Irish people very depressing, though. I would say things are changing now, but when I first arrived people would look at me and, even though they didn't say anything, their eyes would be saying, "What are you doing here? You're here to take money from us." So initially it was very depressing, but I tried to understand their confusion and their attitude towards us; they may fear we want to take over their town and their country. I do think people are changing, that they're trying to accept the fact that we are here. They will get used to us eventually, but they are afraid of change. They are very, very afraid to adapt to their multicultural society but, whether we like it or not, our society is now a multicultural one.

'When I interviewed the Nigerian lady on my show I said to her, "I can't wait to see our kids getting married to Irish kids in the future." And she said, "I have dreamt about that, you know. If it gets to that extent, then it will mean we really accept each other."

'That would speak of integration really well, you know.'

Enda Farrell and Patricia Higgins

whose experiences with
Slí Eile Volunteering
led to their abandonment
of high-flying careers

For some people, their experience of volunteering is so profound that the course of their lives changes forever as a result. They find themselves taking off in a completely different direction than they were previously heading, sometimes even abandoning high-flying careers to pursue an altogether different path. This is precisely what happened to Enda Farrell, who used to be an IT consultant, and Grade A student Patricia Higgins, who had a promising future ahead of her as a management consultant. At the end of a year spent full-time volunteering both turned their backs on 'worldly success' to pursue a kind of lifestyle that they found significantly more fulfilling.

The first time Leitrim-born Enda felt attracted to volunteering was when he was preparing to sit his Leaving Certificate exams and the prospect of going overseas to Africa became very appealing, especially the thought of going before his exams! His mother persuaded him to 'hang in there' despite the fact that he really disliked the pressure he was experiencing during his final year of study. 'I was thinking to myself that the Leaving Cert didn't matter that much because all I wanted to do was go to Africa,' he says. 'It's crazy the amount of pressure on you when you're seventeen.'

Looking back now, Enda would say that the appeal of Africa lay in the fact that it offered 'an escape route' from the stress associated with exams; he genuinely wanted to help overseas, but he also wanted a reason to leave school. In the end he did well in his Leaving Certificate and was lucky enough to be one of ten chosen by Irish Life to go 'straight into the financial world.' Far from 'helping out' in Africa, Enda found himself wearing a suit and tie (which he didn't particularly like), but he was working on computers, which he 'loved'. He was happy enough until one day when he had to attend an insurance seminar. He says, 'They drew a diagram on the board and said, "These are the spheres of what's important to you: at the centre is your family, in the next ring is Irish Life and your friends and in the next, people you know a little bit." I remember thinking it was funny to have Irish Life in the second ring; it seemed a topsy-turvy way of defining what was important.'

Nevertheless, Enda persisted with the work, which he was still enjoying, and he was thrilled when the opportunity arose to do some voluntary work. 'Irish Life used to bring ten children from the inner city away for a week in Wicklow each summer,' says Enda. 'So when I was in my late teens and early twenties I went every summer to do one of those camps. It was nice to help out, but it was also a great break; part of the attraction was that you got to be with five or six of your peers and, when the children were in bed, we'd be able to drink cans and sit around a turf fire. It opened up another world to me: all year we were in our suits and ties in Irish Life, but for this one week we were introduced to something completely different.'

After a few years Enda found himself becoming increasingly dissatisfied with his life as a computer programmer. 'I wasn't happy in it, but when that's your world and all your friends are in it you don't realise there's another world outside,' he says. 'After about five years in Irish Life the economy was picking up and so I decided to self-employ as a contractor, which meant I worked contracts of different lengths in various institutions, like Irish Life, AIB and AOL.'

With the opportunity to do voluntary work with Irish Life gone, it was to be another few years before Enda volunteered. 'In 1998 a paper landed on my desk and it was a Dublin Inner City Trust newsletter looking for IT professionals to do one hour a week in the inner city, teaching computers to adults. I hadn't done any voluntary work for a few years and I decided I would like to do it. So for six months I spent one hour a week teaching basic computing skills in Gardiner Street. It was quite a challenge at first because initially I was quite nervous having to speak in front of ten people; I still remember how nervous I felt giving the first lesson. But the challenge was part of the attraction – as well as sharing my skills I was also pushing myself to stand up in front of people – and it was good for me.'

Having made the move to self-employment Enda's life started to become 'a little bit nomadic'. He decided to 'take a break' from the financial world and, having saved up enough money to go travelling, he proceeded to spend two years exploring Australia and America. 'Because I'd made thousands and thousands of pounds in IT I could just drift. I spent three months cycling across the bush in Australia and I met different people; we would just sit around a campfire talking for hours. I'd assumed most people worked nine to five in an office, but then I met all these people who just spent their time travelling. By the time I returned to Ireland and went back into computers I found I absolutely hated going into work every day. It almost seemed like an unreal world after travelling around the world, meeting so many nomads and drifters. I'd been so free when I was travelling and it was brilliant. After sitting under the stars thousands of miles from anywhere with like-minded people, I felt I was dying in front of the computer screen. I also found I had nothing in common any more with the other programmers. Some of them I knew from the early '90s and I'd be telling them different stories from my travels, but they were moving on to the next stage of buying property, and most of them had long-term partners. That was the start of the break away; I knew something had changed. I had become attracted to the nomadic lifestyle and to new experiences. Sometimes when you're travelling you realise that it really is a gift to be healthy and free, and to have the money to do it. At the time I thought I'd discovered something new, but then I started reading books about the hippy era and I went to eco camps and I discovered that I'm not the only one!

'I was absolutely dying in work. One Monday morning when I went into the office we started to tap away on the computers and the sun was shining on some of the computer screens, so somebody closed the curtains, which made the room very dark. That was it for me, I'd had enough and I resigned four months into a nine-month contract. I absolutely knew I had to because I was dying, otherwise; I had to do it to be true to myself.'

Around that time Enda's attention was caught by a poster he saw in the city centre, which said, 'Are you looking for something different? Do you want to live in a community for ten months?' It was a Slí Eile Volunteer Communities (formerly Jesuit Volunteer Communities) ad looking for young people to volunteer. Enda had 'a huge amount of savings' from his contracts, so he didn't feel it was a financial risk to apply. He was accepted and was given the choice of two volunteering posts – one with the Simon Community, the other working with people with learning disabilities at St John of God's Carmona Services in Glenageary. He decided to go for the latter. For the first three months he volunteered as a classroom assistant in a class of six boys, aged six to ten, with varying degrees of special needs. 'It was like walking into a totally different world,' says Enda. 'The financial industry might as well have been on a different planet. The boys had physical or intellectual disabilities, or a combination of both, and most of their disabilities were quite profound – none of them was verbal, except one boy who had a few words and another who had a little sign language. One or two boys were very frustrated in the classroom and they used to bang on the window. There were two teachers and me, but the kids really needed one-to-one attention. We communicated with them by playing games; we'd also sing songs and they'd clap along and make sounds.

'The main thing I got out of the experience was the feeling that I have a huge gift to have my health, freedom and money, and that, by God, after that I was going to make the absolute most of my life. That's not to reflect negatively on the boys, but it just made me determined to make the most of my gifts. I spent the next few months in Carmona's adult training centre; that was different because most of the people were verbal and had basic social skills. We did reading, writing and art with them and we brought them out on trips. It was probably more fulfilling because there was more communication.'

Enda lived in a community situation with other Slí Eile volunteers, but he didn't feel 'totally free' to pursue the community aspect because he also wanted to spend time with his long-term partner; he therefore felt pulled in two directions. He did enjoy the faith aspect of the community, however, and particularly enjoyed some of the interesting speakers who used to come and talk to the group during a period of reflection each Friday morning. 'We had some very interesting people,' he says. 'I particularly remember a Jesuit priest who had been deported from Chile. We explored different issues as a group, like why we should bother being interested in justice and society. The Jesuits are very much into a practical faith and, although I'm not a practising Catholic, I found that very appealing. I like the Jesuit motto – to find God in all things – I think that's good. A lot of churches seem dead to me now, but I do think the Christian faith means something to me all right; sometimes when I was sitting out in the bush in Australia I'd get a sense that there's more to life than we can see.'

Before signing up with Slí Eile, Enda had read *Awareness* – a book by Jesuit author Anthony de Mello. 'I thought it was absolutely brilliant,' says Enda. 'He was quite open – not very institutionally Catholic – so I kind of knew the Jesuits were slightly alternative; at least, that they don't push the institutional view. Overall, my experience with Slí Eile was life-changing, basically because of the people I met and the situations I was in. I couldn't really look at things the same way again. It helped me discover that there's a huge network out there of people who are into an alternative lifestyle, people who have worked overseas or are involved in the eco- movement or the hippy movement. Most of them don't have very much money, but they're very creative; I enjoy that. I was brought up very strict and Catholic, but I've discovered I like a freer lifestyle.'

The fact that Enda's way of life was moving further and further away from one of 'worldly success' put enormous strain on his relationship with his accountant girlfriend. In the end it took its toll. 'The relationship didn't survive and I suppose that's the negative side of volunteering,' says Enda. 'The more you go into the volunteering world the more you see and the more you change; you start going in a completely different direction. I'd been in a relationship for a very long time: we were thinking of getting married, but then I wasn't earning any money and the wedding was coming up in twelve months, so that was very hard.

'I did one computer contract and then I went travelling for six months to get over the end of the relationship. I went walking through France and Spain: I walked from Paris to the Pyrenees and then to Compastela. I brought a sleeping bag and a mat; sometimes I slept outside and sometimes I stayed in hostels or hotels. It was a fabulous experience because it was everything I love – hard, physical exertion, the outdoors and meeting different people. Walking in France was very solitary (but that was good because I wanted to be on my own at that time), but then I enjoyed meeting different people when I was walking in Spain. There were hundreds of different people coming through every day and so it was a bit like the Canterbury Tales, all the different characters you'd meet.'

On his return to Ireland, Enda went to Cork where he volunteered with the Simon Community. 'It was tough in the homeless shelter because you literally got everything from assault, overdoses and rape to suicides,' he says. 'Sometimes you'd be sitting drinking tea with the residents in the dining room and one of them might say, "Do you have a few minutes?" You'd bring them into a room where you could talk one-to-one and I just used to listen. I'd maybe ask the odd question, but I gave absolutely no advice because I'm convinced that it's very therapeutic for people just to have someone listen to them. A lot of them might have been coming off drink or drugs and were perhaps feeling depressed or suicidal. The most important task for a Simon project worker is to befriend and support the residents and I think just listening to them – especially if they're feeling frustrated or angry – sometimes you can see that seeping away if you just listen to them for fifteen or twenty minutes. It's such a lonely life for them, you know. Savage even. I think the best thing I ever did in the shelter was to shake hands with the residents when they arrived. I'm convinced that gave them something more than all the food and medicine and patching up could do; you could see it in their eyes.'

After six months of voluntary work Enda took a paid position with Simon. 'I actually loved the work and so, for the first time in fourteen years of my working life, I loved going into work,' he says. 'There's no doubt about it; that kind of work brings me happiness. There's a bit of an edge to working with the homeless and drug users, just like travelling is kind of living on the edge. The people in the Simon shelters are cut off physically and socially, just as the people in St John of God's are living on the edge emotionally and socially because a lot of them are isolated. And the one thing I draw from the Christian faith or the gospel is that Jesus calls us to live on the edge. I believe in blind faith, but being sensible at the same time. Many times over the last few years I've just let go of my fears and not worried about the future and so many times people have come out of nowhere to help me do different things. Things just seem to work out when you take a jump.

'I think it's important to be true to yourself. I've been reading the latest book by Gerard Hughes, *God in all Things*, and it's interesting because he says that whatever your deepest, deepest desire is that that is God's will for you. I thought that idea was interesting – that it's not a case of God's will being externally imposed, but it's actually what you really, really want. The idea is that what God really wants is for you to be totally fulfilled and happy. And so my test for any job now is, "Am I happy to get up and go to work on Monday morning? Or do I hate it?"'

Enda reckons his time with Slí Eile provided him with a 'bridge' from the world of computing into the arena of social services. In September 2004 he took up a new post with Simon – this time as a street outreach worker in Dublin. 'Someone once described Simon employees and volunteers as 'adrenaline junkies' because it's so dangerous and exciting. That draws me, the buzz, because I'm always looking for new experiences. Volunteering has changed me because now I think what really, really matters is other people and that you treat other people with respect. I hope I am more sensitive to other people now because I think every person you meet can mean something. That first jump I made from computer programming to Slí Eile was the scariest thing I've ever done; I was terrified, but I absolutely knew it was something I had to do because I would die otherwise. That was the biggest jump and I lost my fear after that; something freed up in me then and nothing will ever be so hard again.'

Patricia Higgins has been involved in voluntary work since her schooldays in Dungannon, Co. Tyrone when she was President of St Patrick's Girls' Academy St Vincent de Paul Society. Her parents never imagined, however, that their extremely bright daughter would do anything other than pursue a business career, as her siblings had done. 'Going to a Catholic school and being in a very Catholic family I had a very strong sense that it would be a good thing to do to get involved with the Vincent de Paul,' says Patricia. 'Being President involved very little, really – just calling the meetings and chairing them – and once a week my friend and I went to visit old people who were bedridden in a hospital ward. It was quite a depressing place in many ways, but one incentive to go was that it was a legitimate way to get out of school early! As well as that, there was some sense that you were doing something good. If I'm blunt, it was something I gritted my teeth to do every week; I really felt for the old people, but as many could no longer talk, I often found myself thinking, "What on earth am I going to say?"'

Patricia had heard about Corrymeela, a reconciliation centre on the north Antrim coast, and decided she would like to make a visit, although it was not so much the interdenominational aspect of the centre that appealed to her at first. 'I knew Corrymeela was a cross-community ecumenical reconciliation centre and that it gave the opportunity to meet members of different denominations, but that wasn't the appeal for me,' says Patricia. 'I didn't grow up gnashing my teeth because I didn't know any Protestants but, going to an all girls school, by the time I was fourteen or fifteen I was gnashing my teeth because I wasn't meeting any boys! I was sixteen when I first went to Corrymeela and it was an amazing experience. I ended up there with five of my closest friends; everybody else who was meant to be in the group had dropped out, so we were these six girls from Dungannon who all knew each other extremely well and we had an amazing weekend. As well as having great craic, we had facilitated discussions about our families, friendships and faith.'

Patricia's initial disappointment at not meeting the opposite sex at Corrymeela quickly disappeared when she discovered there were so many other ways to fill her time there. 'It was a place to swap stories – to hear from others and to be heard myself,' she says. 'It was a place where people tried to put the more positive stuff I'd heard about God into practice. I guess I fell in love with the whole atmosphere; the idea of people listening to each other and the whole concept of sharing and not being challenged. Also the way people pulled together and the craic element; the whole team spirit thing just blew me away. I remember being struck by the decision to wash and reset one hundred and eighty settings for mealtimes, rather than use disposable plates and cutlery – a decision motivated by environmental concerns. It meant more work for the team of volunteers, but given the spirit of the decision, there was a great desire to see it through.'

Given that the Corrymeela experience impacted Patricia 'very strongly', it is not surprising that she returned many times over the next few years – both as a participant and as a volunteer. She attended a Corrymeela 'seed group', which involved six weekends in the year, meeting people from all over Ireland – Catholic, Protestant, unemployed, working, students. As a follow on from that, she spent three weeks as a volunteer at a twin centre in Sweden, which proved a 'fascinating' way to see another country.

After sitting her A-level exams she spent two weeks volunteering at Summerfest, an event held at Corrymeela every two to three years. 'There were three hundred people staying at the centre and I was one of eighteen people helping out, doing everything from erecting tents to washing dishes and keeping the show on the road,' she says. 'I guess I had in the back of my mind that I'd like to go and do a degree and come back and spend a year there. I didn't have a clue what I wanted to do with my life really, but I was really intrigued by Corrymeela. I really wanted to get involved with something like that. I guess the faith-in-action element of it really appealed to me as well as being with like-minded people – people who were fired up by the same kind of things that I like to think I'm fired up by.'

During her four years studying at Trinity College Dublin Patricia's social life revolved much more around the Vincent de Paul Society than with her colleagues in her Economics classes. 'While I struggled with some aspects of Trinity I was anchored in the Vincent de Paul,' she says. 'It quickly became one of my social networks because I was with like-minded people there. I went to visit older people: they were more active than the people I'd visited while I was in school and they were great craic! I helped organise trips and parties for them. It was great. I had to give that up, though, when I became one of the three Presidents in my second year because there was so much to organise and there was a lot of fundraising that needed to be done. We won a Bank of Ireland Society of the Year award in 1993.'

Patricia was not so preoccupied with her volunteering that she forgot to study, however, and in 1995 she was awarded a degree in Economics. She then applied for a job in management consultancy. 'Basically they were asking for all the things I thought I was good at – analytical skills, communication skills and teamwork skills,' she says. 'I had all those, but if I'd looked any further I'd have realised that all jobs ask for those things! But what cemented it for me was that Corrymeela was really key because I wanted to work somewhere like that, but I couldn't see how I'd get there. I didn't know how you got into that kind of work, but I'd heard that the guy who was running it had previously been a management consultant. So I decided that the thing to do was to learn business skills and then to take them out and apply them in the community and voluntary sector. I didn't want to be dismissed as naïve. As the youngest of a family who all went into business I guess that was coming from my own sense of, "OK, I'm not going to go into the business world full-time, but at least I'll be able to hold my own." That was another reason to go for management consultancy.

'I also wanted to find out how to channel goodwill, enthusiasm and energy if it's not motivated by profit. Profit can be criticised for the non-monetary costs it doesn't take into account, but it does have the advantage of being very clear. So how do you enthuse people and make them effective when it's not all about profit? It's easy to rally the troops initially, but how do you sustain that? So I wanted to find out about organisational management development and I understood there would be a chance to do that within the new job. When I took up my post, however, only a few people got to work in that area; the main work new recruits were required for was developing new IT systems for various clients. So I spent two years programming computers, which was essentially a very different area than I had hoped for. It was all about information technology and I was going, "I'm not really a techie". I didn't like the job and I felt I needed out. I was struggling because it really wasn't where I wanted to be. There was a sense that, "I'm not into making mega bucks; sure, I won't refuse them, but it's not the be all and end all" and I had this sense of being really isolated. I had no interest in the work, which was miles removed from what really involved me, and my confidence took a nose dive.

'I considered a few different options and then I signed up to do overseas' volunteering. I was twenty-three and I thought it was time to bite the bullet and stop talking about wanting to do something different and go and do it! But somebody said to me, "That's great you want to work overseas, but what about Ireland? There's plenty wrong here, too." I'd been involved for a number of years in Christian Life Communities, a faith reflection group associated with the Jesuits, and I'd known of Jesuit

Volunteer Communities (renamed Slí Eile Volunteer Communities in 2002), so I decided to apply. I ended up doing voluntary work with them for a year and it was absolutely amazing – the best thing I've ever done! Until then I'd been very good at talking the talk about faith – that's what had appealed to me about Corrymeela – and now I felt it was time to walk the walk, to really put my faith to the test. The gospel says God is with the poor and so I headed out to Ballymun; I parked the car half a mile away the first time because I thought the car would get done in!

'I spent ten months in the Ballymun Drop-in Well Centre and it was just brilliant to break all the preconceptions I'd had in the beginning, to be really accepted and to find a place I loved being in and that I belonged. My dad used to ask me if the women didn't ask what on earth I was doing there. I could honestly say that it rarely came up and, on the contrary, I was very quickly made to feel part of the centre. I was particularly chuffed when, after a big party at Easter, that I had missed, one of the women asked me, "Why weren't you here?"

'The Ballymun regeneration was just coming on stream and I was involved in the day-to-day running of the centre and networking with other groups. We ran re-entry education courses, like flower-arranging, candle-making, drama, music, creative writing, pottery and meditation, and one thing that reflected very well on the centre was that most courses were given by people who themselves had done courses in the centre. The centre's raison d'être was to help young isolated mothers, but the people who it really attracted were women in their fifties or sixties who were now helping to raise their grandchildren, having perhaps already helped to raise their siblings and their own families. They were powerhouses – amazing women who were really resilient and who had light years of life experience. I learnt a huge amount from them.'

Patricia found that spending Friday mornings with the other Slí Eile volunteers and participating in workshops with various speakers was 'amazing'. She says, 'It was great to meet people who were really passionate about peace and justice work, who weren't doing things out of some sense that it was a good thing to do, but who were just really alive and involved. I really envied them because I wanted to be like that. I wanted that core connection they had to Christ and to God and I realised that I didn't have that. I did feel closer to God in Ballymun and I guess some part of me thought I could spend the year volunteering, get that sense of God, take it and put it in my back pocket and then get on with my life.'

In fact, her time with Slí Eile affected her so 'hugely' that it changed Patricia's future plans. 'It gave me a sense of what I really wanted to do and it opened the door to working in that kind of area,' she says. 'It crystallised for me what I'd already experienced at Corrymeela, Vincent de Paul and Christian Life Communities – that sense of a shared vision and commitment to justice. That really got me and I wanted more of that. I was also really lucky to spend that year with great fellow volunteers and I guess it helped me decide who I was and what I wanted. It was like a 'coming out' – a structured way of saying to my friends and my family that this is what I believe in, this is who I am. It helped me in terms of trusting myself and trusting my own instincts, going with the flow and not having to plan everything. At a personal level, it taught me a lot about how to live; I learned to let go of my 'plan'. I didn't know any more where I was heading, but it didn't matter because I was learning to dance (for want of a better word) – to take one step at a time, without having to see where the next step was. I experienced how God can knit together all those seemingly unrelated steps, to reveal a tangible, wonderful answer to long-asked questions and prayers. I realised that all God asks of me is to be prepared to see no further than the next signpost, the next most obvious step. That was huge for me. It gave me the sense that if I really wanted something, I didn't have to worry about how it was going to come about. I could trust to take little steps, knowing that God somehow would weave them together to get me to where He wanted me to be, even though I couldn't plan or foresee where that would be.'

Having a better sense of the type of work she wanted to be involved in, but unclear how best to get there after her time with Slí Eile, Patricia started a Master's in 'Finance in the Community'.

'It was a really bad idea,' she says. 'I thought it would be my doorway into the community world, but I'd got myself into a situation where I was living by myself and studying by myself when what I really wanted was to experience some sense of being involved in a community, not just studying about it. So that went nowhere fast! I gave up after six months when I was offered a job at the Catherine McAuley Centre, which ministers to women in need in the Dublin area. I left after two months, though, when I was offered a job as development officer with Slí Eile; that was a perfect fit for me. They'd never had someone in that post before who had actually spent time as a Slí Eile volunteer. The work involved supporting the full-time volunteers and I loved that; I was consciously very pro the volunteers whenever any decisions were being made, having been on the other side of those decisions at one time. In 2001 we moved from Leeson Street to Gardiner Street and made a commitment to work within the north inner city because on every social indicator it's one of the most deprived areas in the country. I developed a part-time volunteering programme, which involved identifying placements and matching volunteers to these placements. I also had the opportunity to lead a group of volunteers to Zambia for three weeks and that was fascinating; we worked in a hospice, a refugee centre and a school.'

In November 2003, having spent four years in paid employment with Slí Eile, Patricia decided it was time to move to another organisation in order to notch up more management experience. She took up a post as operations officer for Comhlámh – the Irish Association of Development Workers. 'My job involves financial reporting to both our own management and our various funders as well as looking after the IT, payroll and looking at ways we can increase our stream of independent funds from both our membership and from fundraising activities,' she says. 'I realise now that it was a huge thing for me to leave Slí Eile because I'd been involved with them in one way or another since I first came to Dublin at the age of nineteen. One aspect of the job I miss is the opportunity to connect with people around issues of faith and ways in which it can be made relevant to daily life.

During my time in Slí Eile I was invited to give a reflection at the Gardiner Street Gospel Mass a number of times and, while I found it really challenging, I always got a real buzz out of doing it. I welcomed the chance to have to come up with something relevant and coherent to say about the gospel.

'That said, I really appreciate all that I can learn from my current work with Comhlámh. My time in Zambia and some subsequent work on campaigning for debt relief has made me aware of how much work can be done here to make the world a fairer place for all. Working for Comhlámh, I am involved in that work for justice in a wider global sense, and am grateful for that chance. I'm not doing any voluntary work at the moment, as I have been studying theology, which doesn't leave much time, but I look forward to getting back to volunteering at some later time.'

Like Enda, Patricia is in no doubt that Slí Eile changed the course of her life. 'I guess I was always stepping into the business world with the intention of stepping back out again,' she says. 'The volunteer year working in Ballymun was one key experience, but the chance then to work in a professional capacity with other volunteers was a great way to both deepen and develop that experience. I know I would like faith to be an element of my work in the future, but I'm not sure how at the moment; I need to feel my way forward on that one. At least I know now that I don't need to have my whole future mapped out; I can just take it one step at a time.'

Philip McKinley, Vicki Sandall, Bróna Fallon and Adrienne Buffini

whose volunteering overseas, on local radio and with the Dublin Gospel Choir is prompted by their faith

When he was eighteen years old Philip McKinley 'did the backpacker thing' around Europe and, while he enjoyed his time abroad, he had no desire to spend the following summer in the same kind of way. And so when he spotted a Church Missionary Society magazine lying around the kitchen of his family home in the Dublin foothills (his father is rector of Whitechurch Church of Ireland parish) he flicked through its pages and 'became filled with overwhelming thoughts of the world as my oyster'. After giving the matter some thought, he sent an email to the organisation, saying he'd like to go to Africa.

Since he was studying radio and journalism at Dún Laoghaire Institute of Art, Design and Technology at the time, the Church Missionary Society (CMS) decided to send him to Uganda to make radio programmes about some of their projects there. And so Philip spent a month with missionary partners Andrew and Joanne Quill and, much to his delight, he found he was immediately welcomed into the local communities. 'Andrew and Joanne had a CMS car and people used to wave at us, beep their horns and say, "Praise Jesus!" when they saw the car; CMS is so well respected there,' he says.

Philip put together four radio programmes during his stay – one about the Quills' work, one on HIV/AIDS, one on Kiwoko Hospital, which CMS had set up in one of the areas worst affected by civil war, and one about Jonathan Holland – a Dublin man who teaches computing skills in the Luwerro diocese. Four weeks later he returned to Ireland a very different young man. 'The experience left a very, very deep impression on me – a life-changing one,' he says. 'Being exposed to a different culture resulted in a total shift of perspective; it shifted the way I thought about the world, about Ireland, about my community and about my friends and family.

'Uganda is very, very rich in the sense that the community is very strong and sometimes I think going abroad helps you to understand home better. There were no real culture shocks for me going out there, but coming back to Ireland – to see kids hanging out at petrol stations drinking bottles of cider, utterly bored with life – that, for me, was a real culture shock. That sort of thing deeply forces you to question your own society, your own values and your own perspective on life. On my return I noticed people who were materialistic and totally wrapped up in their own culture; I'd never noticed that before.

'The preparation you're given for going to Africa by the media and people's perceptions is that it will be terrible and you'll experience suffering and see flies around black babies; I don't think I ever saw flies around black babies. What you're driven to believe prepares you for the worst and so what shocked me most was that I really enjoyed myself – it was such a wonderful experience. It was a great pleasure, although I'm sure if I'd been working in a hospital or feeding the starving I would have felt shocked. I enjoyed the people, the culture, the music, the sense of community spirit and the church.'

Philip reckons there is no doubt, but Uganda was a real turning point in his life. Instead of pursuing a career in broadcasting, he decided to study theology at Trinity. 'I also took the radical step of signing up to the Vincentian Refugee Centre in St Peter's Church, Phibsboro,' he says, 'And I got involved in leading the youth group here in Whitechurch. I gave talks to different groups about my experiences in Africa and I started playing guitar in churches and schools with an African group, Adun Oyin – things I would have been far too embarrassed to do before. I've always gone to church, but in terms of the development of faith I think there are times when you have epiphanies – and Uganda was definitely a mighty epiphany – it gave a huge jolt to my faith and it made me much more secure in it.'

The following summer Philip returned to Uganda with CMS where he spent three weeks making a video, which has since been shown in schools all over Ireland. He also spent a week in southern Sudan with Archdeacon Henry Leju, who had just returned from a year studying community development at Kimmage Manor in Dublin. In the summer of 2003 Philip spent another four weeks with the archdeacon, much of the time travelling around with him on the back of his motorbike. On this trip CMS had given Philip the task of sorting out a breakdown in communication that had arisen over the building of a community centre (the complete absence of a postal system or telephone network in southern Sudan was making communications difficult). CMS had raised €48,000 for the centre and, during his visit, Philip got to see the first bricks being made. Archdeacon Leju now oversees the running of the centre, which provides information on farming, healthcare and HIV/AIDS awareness as well as providing a meeting place for women's groups, chicken groups and a weaving association.

'Sudan is such a fascinating country, which has suffered terribly from fifty years of civil war,' says Philip, 'Visiting it is a dichotomy of experiences: it both warms the heart and haunts the soul. Through its people, culture and landscape I experienced the truly awesome nature of God's creative power and yet I was so deeply disturbed by the suffering of the people, the indignity of poverty and the evils of war. I saw emaciated children and children with AIDS and leprosy and polio; and there was an outbreak of yellow fever while I was there. I visited refugee camps, which had food distribution but no schools; two were on the banks of the Nile, which floods a couple of times a year. I visited an orphanage, which I heard was raided by the army the following week: all the staff and children were kicked out and they just scattered.

'In Sudan the clergy don't get paid – they're volunteers – and they really live on the breadline. They have incredible pressures because they're expected to lead demoralised communities, which have no resources, and so there's massive pressures on them. I found the worship interesting – you had old people who sang the old hymns and who worshipped the way the missionaries had taught them; and then you had the younger people worshipping in a way which is probably closer to their indigenous culture, using drums and local instruments. It's definitely much more vibrant than the Irish church – much younger and much fresher – and all sections of society are represented.

'For me, it's just been such a pleasure to soak myself in another culture – to try and learn a little of the language and the music – I've fallen in love with the songs. Just to immerse myself into a different way of life is, for me, a very fancy holiday – a very great and a very beautiful holiday. I don't see it as volunteering – volunteering implies too much of the high moral ground, that you're giving your time and your services for the good of other people. I wouldn't do it if I didn't enjoy it, and I do thoroughly enjoy it; it's made such a difference to my life, to my faith, to my relationships and to the way I treat people. It's just turned my head around; that's the only way I can describe it. I guess it's the difference between being a slave to society and being a servant to society; I'm not a hero in any sense. I get great personal happiness out of it and I've made great friends along the way. It gives me great joy and whatever anyone else gets from it is by the by.

'The thing is with Africa there's this great myth that we go out to help; if you're a doctor or a priest, maybe – but no more than helping people here. Africans do not need more help than us; we need just as much help as them – with our relationships and with our social problems. I don't know if I've done anything in particular to help anybody in Africa, but I think it's good that somebody from Ireland goes over and appreciates their culture, shows an interest in the people and shares in the sorrow of the refugees who have suffered so much. And when I return to Ireland I always share my experiences with as many people as I can and try and bring a little enthusiasm into the church here. I think the people who go out to Africa, thinking they have something to give, usually end up burnt out with compassion fatigue. They believe they have everything to give and that the Africans have everything to receive; whereas to learn to receive can be a tricky thing, it can also be very fulfilling. I probably receive much more than I give and a little sacrifice, like going away from family and friends for a month, is the least I can do in return for what I'm given. I would never be so proud as to say I've helped anybody.

'It's always been an absolute pleasure for me to go to Africa – I get so much out of it – and it's been really so wonderful to have refugees, immigrants, economic migrants and foreign students here in Dublin, so I can continue my experiences with Africans. My favourite day of the week is Thursday because that's when I go to the Vincentian Refugee Centre for unaccompanied minors: I help tutor the refugees who attend the homework club there. They're a very talented bunch and they've made a huge impression on me. They're incredible people who have come to Ireland without their parents through all sorts of circumstances. My greatest kick is to put them in touch with something they have an interest in – a football team or a choir – those kinds of things. I love to see them flourishing and their talents being used to the full, complementing Irish people and being used as something positive for society. I also enjoy bringing them up the mountains or to a beach – to give them a bit of life.'

Philip hopes to teach religious education at second-level, which seems a pretty good choice of career, given his track record in tutoring the refugees. The first year he helped a girl with her English studies she ended up getting a higher grade in her Leaving

Certificate English exam than Philip did when he sat the exam three years previously! Philip's involvement in the refugee centre grew out of his membership of the St Vincent de Paul society in Trinity where many students are involved in some kind of voluntary work. He has also been involved in setting up Trinity Voluntary Opportunities and he chairs the One World Society, which deals with issues like debt relief, fair trade, multiculturalism and social justice.

His heavy involvement in all kinds of volunteering beggars the question as to when he gets any study done! But he is quite clear as to why he gives up so much time to his various volunteering interests. 'My motivation all along has been my faith because I think faith has to be something that is socially conscious,' he says. 'It has to make you think of other people. I think if your faith is introverted – if it's all about what Jesus can do for *you* – then I think you really have to question it. The common trap that the pious fall into is focusing on piety rather than society. Jesus was a very socially active man: he preached, but he was also very much hands-on. He preached so much about the Kingdom of God and I think we as his disciples are duly called to enhance this great possibility through our faith and our works. Therefore, I think it's important to walk the walk as well as talk the talk. I would say that volunteering comes from a sense of collective responsibility – a sense that I have something to give to society, although in giving I also receive. I don't think anyone who volunteers should think too highly of themselves, but it is a very rewarding path to lead – a path of enlightenment, learning and discovery. It's made me a happier person and, I hope, a fuller person. And I hope I've much longer to go on this path – that I don't burn out or get distracted or waylaid.'

Whereas Philip's volunteering involves very much 'walking the walk', Vicki Sandall's voluntary work involves 'talking the talk' on her local radio airwaves. For seven years she has broadcast a religious and social affairs programme, *New Horizons*, with Fr Dan Carroll on Radio Kilkenny. They were silenced, albeit briefly, when the station closed in December 2003. Five months later they hit the airwaves again with a similar programme, *Soul Agenda*, on the then fledgling station KCLR96FM (Kilkenny Carlow Local Radio). Vicki says, 'It is a magazine-type programme made up of a lively mix of topical issues with a religious connection, human interest stories (usually with a faith aspect), inter-church debate and matters of local interest.'

Vicki, who is a nurse by training, but who hasn't worked outside the home since the birth of her first child in 1981, devotes up to twenty hours a week researching *Soul Agenda*, as well as preparing for another programme she anchors, *Sunday Matters*. The latter is an integrated programme of contemporary and traditional Christian music, incorporating a reflection time whereby local people are given the opportunity to share something of their faith; there is also a slot where Fr Michael Murphy highlights church news and items of interest in the religious press.

Vicki first became involved in regular broadcasting in 1997 when *New Horizon*'s former presenter, Deirdre Quinn, announced her retirement. As the Presbyterian representative on the station's religious affairs sub-committee, Vicki was involved in looking for a suitable replacement. For one reason or another nobody was willing to step into Deirdre's shoes and Vicki and Fr Dan were asked to 'fill in' until a permanent presenter was found. The pair had absolutely no broadcasting experience bar a one-off programme they had co-presented six months previously. 'We were thrown in at the deep end and we were treading water at the beginning,' says Vicki, 'But we learnt to swim after a while. We continued doing the programme, so either they forgot about us or they couldn't find anyone better! Fr Dan is a very tolerant man and we get on very well; we have our theological differences, which we respect in each other, but we make a good team. On *Soul Agenda* we do our own interviews and we incorporate some banter into the programme, just like we used to do on *New Horizons*. It seems to work.'

Vicki has never looked back since she first entered the studio, throwing herself into broadcasting in a whole-hearted way. She does not hesitate to read newly-published Roman Catholic theological documents if they are going to be discussed on the programme. Over the years she has conducted interviews on limbo, purgatory, hell, indulgences and ecumenism, but her personal preference has always been for human-interest stories. At a local level, she has interviewed a lady who adopted four Russian children, and a recovering alcoholic and his wife about their experiences. Also, a woman who has been in and out of psychiatric hospitals for nineteen years, suffering from depression, and a priest who underwent a heart transplant operation. 'Although we're a local radio programme, I see our remit as being between here and Rome and heaven,' says Vicki. 'I don't see any limits being put on us: our stories are not just of local interest, although there has to be an interest here or there would be no point in doing it. I will talk to anyone who has an experience of God or a strong faith.'

On a national level, Vicki has talked to singer Moya Brennan, Mike Garde of Dialogue Ireland and Gordon Wilson's widow, Joan, from Enniskillen. On the international stage she has interviewed Manchester United chaplain John Boyers, Tory MP Jonathan Aitken (who 'found God' in prison), the German golfer, Bernhard Langer, and an English thalidomide victim*, Brian Gault. She particularly enjoyed talking to a Russian scientist, Professor Dimitri Mustafin, who happened to pick up a Bible on a bookstall outside an Italian university where he was undertaking research. 'He used to get very lonely at the weekends because his family wasn't allowed to go to Italy with him,' says Vicki. 'There was a bookstall outside the canteen and one day he saw a Russian book on it; he picked it up and it was the Bible. To cut a long story short, he became a Christian and he now heads the Moscow Gideons, which distributes thousands of Bibles every year to people in universities and prisons.'

Like Philip McKinley, Vicki's radio work is very much motivated by her faith. 'I see myself as a volunteer on the 'God squad' – as an ordinary person trying to get the gospel across to ordinary people in an ordinary way,' she says. 'I feel very strongly that it is a ministry that God wants me to be involved in – getting the message of the gospel across to those listening in. The difficulty is, though, that radio listeners are not a captive audience; if they don't like what you are doing they will just switch you off. So the challenge is to present what you are doing in an interesting and relevant way.

'There's so many people out there with problems – huge problems – and I genuinely feel that there is an answer to all of those problems. And that answer is God. I honestly and truly believe with all my heart that the answer is to believe and to trust in the Lord Jesus Christ. I see myself as a signpost to that answer and that's why I do what I do; that's what keeps me charged up. To that end I try to do human-interest interviews with people who have themselves suffered, but whose trust in God has brought them through. Now the problems don't go away, but God is there in the midst of them; and that makes all the difference.'

Vicki has never received a cent for her tireless radio work, other than her expenses, but she genuinely does not mind. 'You see, for me it's not about getting paid; instead it's all about sharing the gospel of Christ. Now that sounds awfully pious and I'm not a pious person, but I just feel that it's what I'm called to do. I'm very fortunate that my husband is earning enough money to keep the family, so I don't need to go out and earn a wage packet.'

William is, in fact, hugely supportive and makes suggestions from time to time about possible interviewees or subjects for discussion on *Soul Agenda*. Their offspring, on the other hand – Mark, Jane and Peter – rarely tune in to hear their mum on the radio. 'They're more concerned about whether their clothes are washed and ironed than who Mum's talking to on the radio. To them, I'm just Mum; and the beauty of Mum on the radio is that you can switch her off!'

Even the children, however, had to sit up and take notice when Vicki won a Religious Press Award in 2000. 'They were really chuffed,' she recalls. 'They looked at the award and thought, "Well, maybe there is a bit more to her than not ironing our clothes or not having something decent to eat on the table!"'

Vicki won the award for an interview she did with former UVF leader, David 'Packie' Hamilton. She says modestly that the reason she received it was not because of her interviewing techniques, but because of the interviewee. 'David had been a tough nut, but he found God when he was in prison and it had a huge effect on him,' she says. 'While he was in prison another guy moved in with his wife and beat up David's three-year-old son. A while later the fella ended up in the same prison and David was all set to kill him; he got hold of a knife one day and arranged for the other prisoners to distract the cameras away from him in the exercise yard. He was roaming around in his cell beforehand, trying to psyche himself up to send the guy to eternity, when he felt God speaking to him. He said to God, "Look, you know what this guy has done to my son." And he felt God saying to him, "Well, look what they did to mine." The result was he couldn't get psyched up and he went down to the exercise yard and, instead of killing the guy, David said to him, "Look, I forgive you. God forgave me for what I've done and I forgive you."'

Vicki absolutely loves broadcasting, although she says she has no idea why God chose her. 'It really is rather a hoot because I'm completely unqualified to do the job,' she says. 'But I do know that in the past God has used weak and ordinary people to bring glory and honour to His name. I think God has a tremendous sense of humour: that He opened the door for me, a Presbyterian housewife, to broadcast with two priests! Anybody who knows me knows that I have a tremendous ability for sticking not just one foot in it, but two. And the fact that that doesn't happen every week is down to a lot of prayer and the fact that God's hand is in it. But I'm happy with what I'm doing now; I really am.'

One of the contemporary music groups Vicki has featured on *Sunday Matters* is the Dublin Gospel Choir, which formed in August 2002. The choir members probably don't think of themselves as volunteers, as they all adore singing gospel music, but given the huge commitment involved – twice-weekly rehearsals and up to five gigs a week – it could be seen as a type of voluntary work. After all, the choir members do not receive any kind of payment; any money they make goes towards expenses.

It is because of their love of singing that the choir members make sure to turn up for all their scheduled practice sessions as well as their gigs, which take place anywhere and everywhere – from parish churches to such prestigious venues as The Point and The Olympia. Members come from a variety of backgrounds – there were two refugees among their number, thanks to Philip McKinley (although study commitments have forced them to drop out temporarily as they prepare to sit the Leaving Cert) – but all share one common goal: that is, to express their faith, joy and beliefs through the means of gospel music. They are at home in venues both sacred and secular as they believe gospel music cuts across all boundaries to unite the human spirit wherever people are gathered together.

Adrienne Buffini has loved gospel and soul music 'for years' and had been hoping to join a gospel choir for some time. She first heard the Dublin Gospel Choir when it supported the London Community Gospel Choir at its sell out show in the Helix in April 2003. 'I really thought they were great – even better than the London choir because there was a great oomph from the group,' she says. 'I'd been looking to join a choir, but I didn't know what was around, so I was delighted to come across them. Someone told me they were connected to St Mary of the Angels Church and I looked up the internet to see if I could find out anything; I sent an email to ask if they'd be taking on new members. There were actually auditions the following Sunday and when I turned up I found some people had been waiting three months for the audition to come around, so the timing was perfect for me. A couple of weeks later I heard that I'd got in and I was delighted with myself!'

The fact that it is a huge commitment does not bother Adrienne at all. 'I don't mind giving the time to it because I love it,' she says. 'The gigs, in particular, are great – I just totally love doing them. When I joined, most of the gigs we did were Nights of Soul, which were in different parishes and were set up by Catholic Youth Care. Since then we've sung in the likes of Whelan's and Vicar Street – venues I've often been to because I love live music, but this has been the first time I've had the opportunity to be up on stage. And it's fantastic! Our best gig was probably the night of our launch, which took place in Chief

O'Neill's Hotel in February 2004. We received a standing ovation in the middle of the set (never mind the end!) and that really boosted our confidence.

'We do a lot of charity gigs as well; we sang at a fundraiser for Threshold in the Bank of Ireland Arts Centre and at an Outreach Moldova dinner in Trinity. Shortly before Christmas we performed in the Sanctuary in Stanhope Street – that was a really nice gig – and in Mountjoy Prison. None of us knew what to expect there; we thought we might get heckled a lot and we'd been told just to keep on singing and to keep our eyes on the conductor. In fact, it went really well and there was a great reception; I think they were quite surprised by us. They were all quite upbeat in the men's training unit (pre-release prisoners) because they knew they were getting out soon, but the women's prison was more hard going – Christmas must be such a tough time for them. But it certainly felt like a rewarding thing to do.'

Adrienne would not describe herself as a regular massgoer, but faith is certainly an important aspect of her singing. 'I suppose you wouldn't really be singing gospel music if you didn't have a belief in God,' she says. 'Not that I'm very religious, but I try to treat everyone in a good way and I suppose that's the gospel message. I certainly do believe in God and I'd say singing in the choir has helped my faith. Some of the songs are very touching; you can't help but think, "Wow, that's a lovely message!" I just love gospel music – the power behind it and the way it comes across.'

Bróna Fallon, who conducts the choir, started singing in the St Mary of the Angels choir in 2000 and stayed with the choir when it re-formed into the Dublin Gospel Choir two years later. Like Adrienne, she finds the experience of singing gospel music has enhanced her faith. 'It's definitely a combination of the music and the words,' she says. 'Some of the slower songs, in particular, have so much meaning behind the words. I don't go to mass outside of choir – I'm not into the institutionalisation of religion – but I would consider myself very spiritual. Maybe that's a cliché in the modern day, but I'm moved so much by the music and I totally believe in God. I think it's a direct kind of faith because it's about how I act and what I feel rather than about having to go to church. Some of the songs still give me goosebumps, even though I've sung them hundreds of times; I've been close to tears on a number of occasions because I've been moved so much.'

Singing at mass is quite different from performing at a gig; for a start, the songs chosen for mass tend to be slower and quieter. 'You get a different sort of crowd at mass compared to somewhere like Vicar Street,' says Bróna. 'We wouldn't move as much at mass as we do at our gigs; we tone it down a little because we have to cater for people who have been coming to church for maybe twenty, thirty or forty years. The gigs are a different story – we let loose and just let everything go mental – and the audience really reacts to that and they join in. From the beginning we try and get people involved – dancing, moving and singing along. Some people don't feel comfortable getting up and letting loose, but the majority of people react very well. Sometimes I'm amazed: we'll go into a place where you think you won't get much reaction and by the end of the night everyone is literally screaming for more. They're on their feet, giving us standing ovations, dancing in their seats and everything. I don't know how it happens, but it does!'

Bróna used to share the conducting with fellow choir member, Orla McGowan, but now Bróna does all the conducting and organises the rehearsals while Orla teaches new songs and works out the harmony lines. Bróna has had absolutely no training in conducting, but she has a wealth of singing experience, first joining a choir at the age of nine. 'Basically I let the rhythm of the music guide me,' she says. 'I've never had formal training, but it seems to work. So far so good!'

There is no doubt about it: Bróna, Adrienne and their fellow choir members are certainly doing something right because the name of the Dublin Gospel Choir has become high-profile very quickly. They are now in the position of giving workshops to other gospel choirs in an attempt to provide others with the kind of support and encouragement they themselves have received from the London Community Gospel Choir. They have performed at such high-profile events as the Meteor Awards in

The Point and the opening ceremony of the Special Olympics in Croke Park and they have even recorded with no less a group than The Hothouse Flowers, accompanying the band on its latest album, *Into Your Heart*. January 2004 saw the choir appearing on *The Late Late Show* and *Open House* with The Hothouse Flowers as well as performing in The Olympia, HMV, Tower Records and Celtic Note. 'It was nerve-racking singing on *The Late Late Show*,' admits Bróna. 'My whole mouth was shaking from nerves and I kept thinking, "Please don't let the camera be on me". It was great publicity, however, and we're so much more in demand now; our name is really getting out there.'

There seems little doubt that the Dublin Gospel Choir is going from strength to strength and Adrienne and Bróna both see themselves continuing with the group for a long time to come. 'I'll be singing with the choir for a good number of years,' says Adrienne. 'There's no end in sight for me! I used to be a terrible one for starting a class and giving up after a week or two, but I turn up at choir practice and gigs every time – whatever the weather – because I really enjoy it.'

'I'll definitely continue to be involved for the foreseeable future,' agrees Bróna. 'It's hectic at times – as well as rehearsals and gigs, I have music team meetings to attend, rehearsal team meetings and management team meetings, but I don't mind because once we start singing I get totally absorbed in the music. It's a great buzz! As soon as we start singing and the crowd reacts to us and they react to the music, it snowballs into a huge amount of energy. I can't describe it – it's like as soon as I'm out there something takes me over and I'm totally lifted above everything. It's incredible – whether we're singing at a mass or a gig, it doesn't really matter – the feeling is the same.'

*Thalidomide: a drug formerly used as a sedative but found in 1961 to cause foetal malformation when taken by a mother early in pregnancy. A child born deformed from the effects of thalidomide.

Christine Denner and Geraldine Toner

*who collect shoeboxes
packed with toys and
clothes and bring them
overseas to give to
poor children*

When Geraldine Toner first heard about Operation Christmas Child seven years ago, she immediately wanted to know more. Her cousin, Louise Ward, who was involved in the scheme, explained that it was really quite simple. All you had to do was wrap a shoebox and then fill it with toys and clothes, and send it to a child in a poor country who would otherwise receive nothing at Christmas. Without hesitation, Geraldine assured Louise that she would make up a few boxes.

In fact, she enjoyed doing it so much that she ended up producing no less than twenty shoeboxes! The following year she made up more boxes and invited her family, friends and colleagues to do the same. Having told them they could drop their shoeboxes at her house, she ended up with seven hundred piled from floor to ceiling in the hall and up the stairs of the house she shares with her husband and their three children in Dublin's north inner city.

To avoid having a congested house the following autumn, she asked her boss in Dublin City Council for permission to collect the boxes in a disused room in the council's Buckingham Street premises. He gladly granted her permission to do this in the short-term. In fact, the depot soon became known as The Shoe House and Geraldine used the same room for the next five years. Just as well she was no longer storing the boxes at home because the number of shoeboxes dramatically increased, with a total of 8,500 collected in 2002. In 2003 the premises were unfortunately no longer available, but Geraldine was offered the use of a room in a community centre two days a week. This was far from ideal and it certainly didn't help matters when burglars broke in one night, ripped open the boxes and poured beer over their contents. Not surprisingly, Geraldine is currently on the lookout for more secure premises for the collection of boxes for Christmas 2004.

Over the years Geraldine has become increasingly efficient and now has a management committee, consisting of herself and three friends – Mary McCann, Marianna Page and Marie Byrne – who have also become involved in the project. She reckoned it would be a good idea to share the workload, especially as she had no desire to neglect her other responsibilities (she works full-time as the council's environment manager for the north-east inner city and there is also her family to consider). Her husband, Jude, is a tremendous help to her – he minds the children while she is busy with shoeboxes and, when she's at home, he collects boxes from schools and various organisations.

Operation Christmas Child takes up a remarkable amount of Geraldine's time, starting with a couple of hours a week in September and gradually building up to twenty-plus hours in November. 'I start in September by doing, maybe, one evening a week and it grows from there,' she says. 'It gets to the stage where I seem to be thinking about shoeboxes every minute of the day. It takes a lot of work and it completely takes over my life for a period every year; I used to go straight from work to The Shoe House and I'd be there until ten o'clock every night. It winds down in December, when all I have left to do is administration and lodge the money. By the time Christmas comes I'm sick of sheboxes and I hope never to see one again, but I know that by the time the next September comes I'll want to do it all over again!'

So, why exactly does she keep doing it? 'When you see videos of the children receiving the boxes and you know that they are the only presents those children will get at Christmas, it makes it all worthwhile,' she says. 'And when you see all the boxes piled up in the depot and the vans come to collect them and there's thirty or forty crates full of shoeboxes going out, then you do feel that it's worth it. I know that if I was a kid and I had very little and somebody handed me one of these boxes I would be so thrilled. I just feel that it's such a simple idea and if everyone in Ireland filled a box, it would be so great. When we have so much, it's such a small thing to do.'

Geraldine was asked to go on a trip to deliver boxes in 2001, but an untimely illness prevented her from going; so she was thrilled to be asked to join a team going to Croatia in December 2003. Although she was 'a bit nervous' about witnessing poverty, she 'jumped' at the offer. 'It was the most humbling trip I've ever done,' she says. 'The people are very, very poor – they have absolutely nothing – and yet they have no bitterness; they don't in any way feel hard done by. You'd go into their homes and they'd be dressed in their Sunday best and they'd make biscuits for you because they'd just be so glad to be visited. A lot of families don't even get state benefit and they're literally living on nothing. You don't see any litter because nothing gets thrown away; everything gets reused and, at the end of the day, if something can't be used it will be used as firewood. One house we went into had last year's shoeboxes on top of the cupboards and they were being used for storage. The shoeboxes are shipped in crates and in another house we saw lots of the previous year's crates pinned to the wall and hammered onto the ceilings for insulation.'

The trip to Croatia really brought home to Geraldine the impact that the shoeboxes have on the children who receive them. 'The children had very few toys and when you gave them a box it was just as if they'd fallen into Aladdin's cave,' she says. 'Even a balloon, a pack of bobbins or a packet of sweets would bring such glee to their faces; they were just so glad to receive a gift. And they were so well behaved! When we visited a refugee camp the children sang and recited poems to us and it was an hour and a half before they were given the shoeboxes. They all came up to receive their boxes in an orderly fashion; there was no pushing, shoving or grabbing.'

Geraldine will never forget her time in Croatia and she would love to make a return trip in another couple of years. 'We saw that there were still bombed out buildings in Zagreb and that the train station was non-existent,' she says. 'I'd like to go back eventually and I'd hope to see some of the buildings built up; it seems as though it's become a forgotten territory, with places like Iraq and Afghanistan getting all the attention now. We heard a lot of horrific stories, but people were just so delighted that we had gone to visit them. It was a very humbling trip and I was delighted I'd gone. Giving out the boxes really makes you think about what we have in Ireland and what we give our kids; and it makes you think how much love has gone into each box.'

Christine Denner also collects shoeboxes in north Dublin, collecting no less than 2,200 boxes in her Raheny home when she first became involved in 2001. 'It was unbelievable,' she remembers. 'I used to come in from work in the evening and there could be ten messages on the answering machine, asking me to pick up boxes. Before I'd even make dinner I'd be ringing people, organising pick-ups. My husband, Philip, and I used to sit up till one o'clock in the morning checking boxes and I remember feeling absolutely exhausted by the time Christmas came. I was more organised the following year and I got the use of a warehouse – we did over 7,000 boxes then – and last year we did 9,700. So it's increased quite a lot, but I have more people on board to help now. I know a few people with vans and they do pick-ups from schools; you could get up to seven hundred boxes from the larger schools and I can only fit about 130 boxes in my car (that's without being able to see out)!'

Like Geraldine, Christine felt somewhat apprehensive when she was asked to go overseas to help deliver shoeboxes. 'I kept thinking about all the unknowns,' she says. 'I'm an organised person – I like to know what's happening and I need time to prepare myself. I was asked to go to Armenia in January 2004 and it was difficult because I had no idea what to expect. But the response of the Armenian people was just unbelievable and it was a wonderful experience; I'd go back again tomorrow. I feel I benefited more from the people we visited than they did from us; I really felt so humble that they thought we were these wonderful people, whereas all we were doing was delivering boxes on behalf of the kids back in Ireland.

'Armenia is a very bleak country – very drab and colourless with lots of rundown buildings – and I think the saving grace, for me, was that there was snow (I love snow). A lady who runs a nursery school told us we'd no idea what a difference the shoeboxes made to the kids. And it's true. We have no comprehension, really, because kids in Ireland have so much in comparison. The children there don't have TVs or gameboys or any of the stuff our kids take for granted; and yet they seemed very content. For some children, the shoebox is the only thing they ever receive; some opened the boxes, looked at what was inside and handed them back because they had no concept that it was theirs to keep. Some of them laughed hysterically when they were given a box, some cried and others were just amazed. Even something like a toothbrush is exciting for them because they might be used to sharing a brush with their whole family. I know our kids would hate to get a toothbrush or a bar of soap for Christmas!'

The group distributed shoeboxes in schools, orphanages and refugee camps; after the war with Azerbaijan refugees, many people have made their homes in abandoned buildings, including disused prisons and water tanks. Not surprisingly, conditions there were bleak and very basic. One school they visited was 'appalling'; there was no colour and no pictures on the walls and the toilets were literally just holes in the ground. A state-run orphanage they visited, on the other hand, was in a remarkably good state of repair. 'It was just beautiful,' says Christine. 'It had dorms with beautiful wooden bunks and hand-knitted quilts on the beds and the classrooms were warm and cheerful and had pictures everywhere. My daughters had made up shoeboxes and, while Miriam had sent hers off anonymously, Natalie wanted me to pick out a girl to give hers to. I saw this particular girl in the orphanage and she seemed a little bit shier than the other kids and I got this feeling that I'd like to give the box to her. I went and chatted to her – her name was Gayanah – and I gave her the box; it was all very emotional.'

Christine found the atmosphere in the prison refugee camp very warm and friendly, which was in stark contrast to the water tank camp. She put this down to the regular visits made by members of Christian Cultural Ministries, an organisation set up by an evangelical pastor called Ashosh, with whom the group was staying. Although Armenian, Ashosh was in fact born in California; the family returned to Armenia some years ago when Ashosh's father, John, felt God was calling them back to their native country. 'John drove us around in his car and, although he is eighty-five, he looks thirty years younger,' says Christine. 'He used to say to us, 'I still have work to do for God and He keeps me young'. Their hospitality was amazing and they clearly have such a heart for the people, especially the poor and the needy. Ashosh runs a TV station and he broadcasts Christian programmes; he also founded a church that regularly sends teams of people to the prison refugee camp to bring them food parcels and talk to them about Jesus. Seeing the difference this has made to the lives of the refugees, the government gave the church land to build a centre which is used for Bible studies, Sunday School and activities for the kids. The atmosphere in that place was totally different to the water tank camp; it was unbelievable.

'I know God works in Ireland today, but I feel so often we don't let Him because it's easy for us to put our hands in our pockets. But a lot of those people have to live by faith because they don't have the financial resources we have. They all seemed very content; even though they had very little materially, they had a peacefulness and a joy. It wasn't like a resignation – it was like as if there was hope there. And I feel that the people from the church have imparted hope to them in the fact that they believe

Jesus can make a difference to people's lives. I didn't see that kind of hope in all the people I saw in Armenia, but I certainly saw it in the refugees I met in the prison camp. In Ireland we have so many distractions in our lives – we're so busy and we have so much materially – that it's very easy to leave God out because we have resources and we know we can do things on our own. But over there people have nothing and they have to depend on God.

'One place we went to when we looked at the number of shoeboxes we'd brought and we looked at the number of kids waiting for boxes and we thought there was no way there was enough boxes for all the children. And so we prayed. I remember just saying, "Lord, please do a loaves and fishes multiplication here; we have no-one to depend on, but You." There were guys on the stage handing out boxes to the children and they just kept handing them out until every single child had a box. And they had some boxes left over!'

Christine describes herself as a committed Christian and it is clearly her faith that motivates her involvement with Operation Christmas Child. 'The Bible asks if your faith doesn't lead you to want to do something, is it dead or alive? And Samaritan's Purse was set up based on the parable of the Good Samaritan where Jesus said, "Go and do likewise". As a Christian I believe I have been commissioned to go and do good. Yes, we're called to bring the gospel of Jesus into our everyday lives, but we're also called to go the extra mile. I suppose, for me, it's a chance to put my faith into action and to give back some of what God has given me to people who are less fortunate.

'My girls were quite upset when I told them I was going to Armenia because they could see from the map that it's quite near Iraq; they were very concerned that I wouldn't come back. We had a chat and I explained to them that I had to do it because I felt it was what God wanted me to do. I said they would have to believe that He would look after me; I also said that they needed to pray for me while I was away because, as well as that being good for me, it would also be good for them. It would give them strength because they would know that God was listening to them and He would give them peace as they prayed.'

Christine believes Operation Christmas Child is not only good for the recipients, but also for the children who wrap and fill the shoeboxes. 'I think the idea is very good in that kids are encouraged to give,' she says. 'And they know that the boxes are going to poor children. Most of them see a video about the project and I think this has an impact on them, especially seeing the look on the faces of the children when they receive the boxes. A lot of schools make it a decent kind of project for pupils to do.'

Every autumn Christine and Geraldine contact schools, clubs and organisations in north Dublin and invite them to wrap and fill shoeboxes. If they're interested and they haven't done it before Geraldine, Mary McCann or another volunteer will visit them to explain what is involved. 'We show them the easy way to wrap a box (because there's an easy way and a hard way to do it!) and then we have a chat with them,' says Geraldine. 'We tell them the kinds of things that are good to put in the boxes and we show them the video of children receiving shoeboxes.

'Women's groups are particularly interested. A group of about a dozen senior citizens meets in the Summerhill Centre on a Wednesday night and they spend all the winter months covering boxes and collecting fillers so that the boxes will be ready for the next Christmas. They use their pension to buy one or two items each week. It gives them something to do in the winter months – especially senior citizens, who mightn't have much contact with other people. The North Wall Women's Centre on Sheriff Street has a group of young mothers who are early school leavers; they have very low self-confidence and yet they make absolutely magnificent boxes.'

Geraldine never fails to be overwhelmed by people's generosity. 'Dublin people are so generous, it's unbelievable,' she enthuses. 'Some of the boxes are absolutely magnificent and so much thought has gone into them; some are overflowing because there's so much in them. The best boxes contain a little bit of everything; there's no point filling a box with all clothes or all toiletries. A box should have some clothes – a hat, scarf and gloves or a pair of socks – also, some toiletries and a few small toys, like dinky cars, a ball, a skipping rope and paper and pens.

You have to think, "If I was a child getting this box, what would I like in it?" It just takes a little bit of thought.'

Geraldine may well be fed up with the sight of shoeboxes by the time Christmas comes, but it is never too long into the New Year before she starts thinking about them again. 'I don't drink and I don't smoke, so if I've a few bob to spare I buy fillers for the boxes,' she says. 'I spend a little bit every week and I just store the items until October when it's time to make the shoeboxes again. I buy things from the Pound Shop during the year and if I see anything reasonable in the sales I buy them as fillers.'

In fact, Geraldine never lets a good opportunity pass. One day – when she heard that Penny's in Artane was selling baseball hats at the bargain price of ten for €2 – she gave a senior citizen from a local club the money she had in her purse and asked her to go and buy as many as she could. 'The staff probably thought the woman was mad when she bought eight hundred baseball hats,' laughs Geraldine. 'We then added a cap to each of the boxes that didn't already have a hat. And we have lots left over, which we'll use next year.'

Every single box has to be opened so that its contents can be checked by Geraldine or one of her cohorts. 'We make sure there isn't anything in the box that there shouldn't be – like sharp objects, marbles, bubbles (they could burst and spill) or any battery-operated items or war toys. A lot of people put in Action Men, but we can't send them. Nothing ever gets thrown out, though – the things we have to remove from the boxes either go to a Sunshine Home or a charity shop. We add sweets to any boxes that don't have any already. Some of the local shops in the north inner city donate sweets to us – one shop last year gave us 250 boxes of them. Some people in the area might not do a box – someone, say, with arthritis might not be able to wrap a box - but they will give us a few items in a bag to add to boxes. So people are very generous.'

Operation Christmas Child really is a community effort. When she goes to Mass Geraldine often finds a pile of wrapped and filled shoeboxes waiting for her at the back of the church and people often stop her on the street and ask her to collect boxes from their home or place of work. Offers of help are always gladly seized. 'There was a woman from the East Wall whose granddaughter had done a box and she accompanied her granddaughter to the depot, when she was delivering the box, because she was so fascinated by the whole idea. I asked her if she had half an hour to spare and she ended up spending the next three evenings with us, helping us to check the boxes as they came in. She was delighted because she said she was always looking for things to do in the winter. I'd never met her before, but now she's on my list for next year!'

Sarnat Bennett, a teacher in Central Model Infant School in the north inner city first heard about Operation Christmas Child in 2001. She thought the scheme was 'a great idea' and asked her first class pupils to help her fill fifteen boxes. In 2002 she extended the scheme to other classes with the result that the school filled about fifty boxes in total.

Knowing that some of her pupils came from households where money was probably tight, Sarnat felt it was too much to expect each pupil to fill a box. 'I sent home leaflets about the scheme and asked if the children could bring in any suitable items,' she says. 'I just asked them to bring in anything they could, even one item, – and I asked for empty shoe boxes and Christmas wrapping paper because some of the children's parents work on the stalls in Henry Street, selling wrapping paper. About ten children brought in boxes which were already wrapped and filled; the others brought in shoeboxes, wrapping paper and clothes and toys, which we collected in a big crate. The children took turns to wrap boxes and fill them; they decided whether a box was for a boy or a girl and then chose appropriate items from the crate. They really, really enjoyed doing it.

'A lot of the class are very poor and when I introduced the idea some of them came up to me on the side and said that they wouldn't have anything to bring in because they didn't have any toys themselves. One child, who is homeless, was upset that she would not be able to bring anything in, but in the end she got really into wrapping and filling the boxes; it was a real confidence-boost for her. She made cards to put in the boxes and it really gave her a sense of achievement. So it was a great chance for all of them, even the poorer children, to feel that they were helping in some way.'

Megan Mangan's uncle gave her money to buy toys to fill three shoeboxes, which she wrapped and filled at home – one for a baby, one for a girl aged six and another for a boy aged six. Sandra Olaiwola put teddies, Digimon monsters and a doll into the box she made and is looking forward to filling another box next Christmas. 'It's a good idea so that the children who get the boxes can have lots of fun at Christmas, like us,' she says. 'The children are very poor and we want Christmas to come to them, too.'

Dean Byrne bought a toy tiger cub with his pocket money, which he put in a box along with a puppet, a teddy, a tennis ball and hat, scarf and gloves. 'We were very busy making boxes like Santa's little elves,' he says. 'We're going to have a good Christmas and we wish the poor children would have a good Christmas too.'

So, will Megan, Sandra, Dean and their classmates wrap and fill more shoeboxes next year? 'Oh yes!' they cry in unison. 'We can't wait to make more.'

Pupils from John Scottus and Sancta Maria in Dublin and St Joseph's in Nenagh

who lent a helping hand as classroom assistants, art therapists, street sweepers and 'brickies' in Africa and India

The Irish education system has come a long way since the days when its primary focus was on the three 'Rs' (reading, writing and arithmetic). With the introduction of subjects like Civic, Social and Political Education and Social Personal and Health Education, pupils are now encouraged to think beyond the world of academia. It is now standard practice, particularly during transition year, for pupils to become actively involved in the community and sometimes even to venture overseas to lend a helping hand in a developing country. The latter experience often turns out to be so life-enhancing that students find themselves returning to Ireland with the feeling that they have almost certainly gained more from the trip than those they were seeking to 'help'.

In February 2003, seventeen pupils from the John Scottus School, Donnybrook headed out to Calcutta for three weeks where they spent their mornings building a playground and assembly hall for a village school and their afternoons helping street children with their homework. 'It all seems like a dream now because it was just so different over there,' says Niamh Griffin. 'First of all, when we got off the plane we were hit by the heat, it was just like somebody had opened an oven door and the airport was horrible. Then, going on the bus to the school where we were staying, what really hit me was that everyone looked so poor; there were just heaps of people rushing about, there was rubbish everywhere and there was this smell of egg and onion. And it was like bumper cars the way they drove; they drive on both sides of the road and there were no traffic lights, but everything stops if a cow walks onto the road. It definitely was a culture shock.'

Niamh's mother, Siobhán, who was one of seven adults to take part in the trip, admits she was 'in a bit of shock' when they first arrived. 'There were people constantly moving on the streets and I felt that if I just stepped outside the convent gate I would get swallowed up and nobody would ever see me again. There was all this kind of madness on the streets and when the bus drove in the convent gates it was peaceful. Really peaceful. Niamh wasn't feeling well when we arrived – she hadn't eaten and somebody said I could get her a banana from one of the street traders – but I said, "I'm not going out into that madness; if I do, I'll never come back". That was my first impression, but little by little we did venture further afield.'

The group was staying in the Loreto Convent, Sealdadh, which is run by Sr Cyril Mooney, who is originally from Co. Wicklow, but who has spent the past twenty-five years in India. Before they went out the group had been told that the school had a 'new block', so they weren't too concerned about their accommodation. Until they got there, that is. The ten girls had to sleep on mats in one classroom, the seven boys in another; although it was dusty, the pupils were happy enough with that arrangement. They weren't too impressed, however, when they saw the bathroom facilities – the toilet was a hole in the ground and there was no shower. 'We washed in a bucket of water,' says

Sinéad Collins. 'There was a tap at knee level and cold, brown water came spluttering out; we used a jug to pour the water over us.'

An hour's bus journey took them to the village school and there they came in for a further shock when they discovered the kind of work they would have to do. 'We had been told we were going to be filling in a small pond in front of the girls' school and building a wall, in order to make a playground for them because the school was surrounded by paddy fields and they had nowhere to play,' says Sinéad. 'When we got there we discovered the "pond" was actually huge – sixty foot by eighty foot and ten foot deep! The first day we organised this massive human chain of about two hundred people – some girls from the school and some villagers came to help us – and so we started to dig and we passed along buckets of soil to fill in the pond. We worked all day and there was still a huge "pond" by the end of it.'

Much to everyone's relief, after a few days some trucks came and filled in the pond with rubble, which meant the group could get on with their next task, which was to build a wall. 'By the end of the three weeks the wall was finished,' says Niamh. 'We also built six twenty foot pillars and they planned to add on a roof after we left, in order to make an assembly hall. We had great craic doing it and we all bonded so well, but it was hard work and we were always dying for our breaks and dying to go home.'

After returning to the convent for lunch the group used to head to the classrooms to assist the teachers and then, when classes had finished, they'd go up onto the roof where some street children live – they sleep on mattresses there and they have lockers to store their few possessions. 'Sr Cyril takes these children in – she calls them The Rainbow Children – and they range in age from three to eighteen,' says Niamh. 'They can come and go as they please, but usually they end up living there. Her main aim is to educate the children, so that they will stay off the streets. Right from the first day they were all over us – they were up on our laps, playing with our hair and calling us 'auntie' or 'uncle'. We each had one or two children who we gradually got more friendly with.'

'We mainly helped them with their homework, but we also played games with them,' says Joanna Pierce. 'There was one girl who said she'd like to write stories and so we wrote stories with her. We write letters to them now and they write to us. I'd love to go back and see them again, but I think I'd find it hard.'

The students experienced a wide variety of emotions during their trip, both highs and lows. 'I don't know how you could go out there and not be affected,' says Joanna. 'You'd trip over something in the train station and you'd realise it was a body. The place was just covered with people sleeping; and on the streets as well. There were people horribly deformed – lepers and people with missing limbs. We visited Mother Teresa's home for sick children and we all came out crying; there were all these children in cots, just lying there. They were happy to see us, though, and if you just held their hand for a while they were so happy. I know it maybe sounds a bit clichéd, but I think we all grew up while we were out there.'

The students had been warned not to give money to anyone they met; and if they did, that they would quickly find themselves surrounded by beggars. Sr Cyril had also advised them, if any children approached them, to just say, 'Go to school' (at school they receive food as well as education). The advice wasn't always easy to follow, however. 'One girl did give money to a lady and she was glad she did because the woman's face just lit up,' says Sinéad. 'I remember walking by some lepers outside the temple and I felt so angry with myself for walking past them; I've beaten myself up about it since.'

The trip had a profound effect on all the participants – none more so, perhaps, than Sinéad. 'It made me realise what I want to do with my life now,' she says. 'I want to be a secondary school teacher and I want to spend my summers in India teaching. I definitely want to go back there. I want India to be a part of my life; I really, really do.'

Niamh's career choice has also been influenced by the trip. 'When I went to India I wanted to be an interior designer, but having seen what education can do I now want to be a primary school teacher. Initially, I thought the street children wanted an education so that they could get a job and have a career, but while we were there it became clear that they valued education for its own sake; they were simply hungry for knowledge.'

Siobhán reckons the trip was 'fantastic' for everybody – parents, pupils and teachers alike. 'We could have gone out there with an arrogant attitude of "We're going to help", but you know, even though they had so little they taught us so much.'

The eight pupils and three teachers from St Joseph's Christian Brothers School, Nenagh who went out to Zambia in April 2003 were also deeply affected by their experiences. They were based in a small town called Mazabuka, which consists of two proper roads, the rest being dirt tracks. The only other white people they saw during their two-week stay were the Christian Brothers and the Sisters of Mercy nuns who live there. 'The brothers and sisters run everything in Mazabuka,' says Shane Cullinane. 'They run the schools, the health clinics, the hospitals and a centre for people with disabilities. We got to visit everywhere at some stage during our trip and so we got a taste of everything.'

The students, who went out as part of a Christian Brothers' developing world immersion project, had to sleep on mattresses on the floor of a community hall. 'It was fine, apart from the lizards,' says Shane. 'The centre was the gathering place of the villagers and they'd put on cultural shows for us every evening. It was amazing. The sisters provided food and some of the local women cooked it for us. Most nights we were given some mealy meal, which is the staple diet of the Zambians – it's like semolina, very tasteless – but they also cooked us beef, rice and sausages. We were stunned by the quality of the food we were given.'

A couple of Christian Brothers stayed with the group in the community hall. 'They listened to what we had to say and they told us their stories,' says Christopher Comerford. 'They also prayed for us. We had a group reflection every night, which gave everyone the opportunity to get something out of their system; these were really helpful because some parts of the trip were really, really tough. We visited a prison and it was honestly one of the worst things I've seen in my life; it was pretty much a compound with a few rooms coming off it. It had been built for thirty people, but we saw one hundred and twenty people, just sitting out in the open.'

The students took turns to lead the periods of reflection. 'We would just pick an event from the day, like the trip to the prison or one of the schools anything that struck us, and we'd talk about it,' says Shane. 'If you brought something up then everybody else might say, "Oh, yeah, that hit me as well", so you knew you weren't the only one. When we went to the prison, in typical Zambian style they all sang for us, every prisoner just belted out this tune. It was unbelievable. We'd heard they're mad about football in Zambia and so we gave them a football and they really appreciated it.'

David McCann was particularly struck by the women's part of the prison. 'It was just one room and in it there were six women and their children,' he says. 'There was a thin mattress on the floor and the room was almost pitch black. There was a small bathroom, but you couldn't see anything when you first walked in because there was no lighting. We discovered that no food had come into the prison that day and so one of the nuns went and bought a bag of maize, so they'd have something to eat. If she hadn't done that, the prisoners would have had nothing to eat all day.'

The students also visited a number of schools to help out as classroom assistants. 'The children were always so happy, smiling and singing,' says Christopher. 'Whenever we went into a classroom the teacher would stop the class and the children would all sing a song to welcome us! The kids were so friendly and interested in what we had to say; they'd keep asking questions and they'd have kept us talking all day, if they could.'

'The teachers would guide us in what to do,' adds Shane. 'We talked a lot about Ireland and the kids asked us very intelligent questions about our population and politics. We were stunned by the questions they asked us.'

The Nenagh teenagers were struck by the poverty they saw all around them. They noticed that most people walked barefoot; evidently they could not afford to buy shoes. 'You'd see the children bringing bottles of mealy meal and water home from school,' says Christopher. 'They are given one meal a day in school, they eat half of it and then bring home the rest. It's unbelievable when you think about how much food we waste. When you're living in Ireland you don't have to think about what's going on in the rest of the world, but when you go over there you realise these things are actually happening. It's not just on the TV any more; it's right there in front of you. The trip really taught me to appreciate what I have; the people we met had nothing and yet they came out of their mud huts every day shining and smiling and so happy with what they had. If you gave them a present of something small, like a football or a tennis ball, they were so happy.'

Shane says the trip was tough at times, 'there were ups and downs', but that he has learned from the experience. 'Everyone asks how it's changed us and you're dying to tell them, but you can't,' he says. 'It's very hard to put words on it. OK, I do appreciate things more now, but it's not just that. I really had to admire the nuns; they're some of the strongest people I've ever met. I'm hoping to go back after I finish college; if not to Zambia, then to another developing country.'

David says he, too, no longer takes for granted his western lifestyle. 'Seeing the poverty in Zambia made me realise what we have and how much we take for granted here,' he says. 'When I see someone throwing out food now I think, "Why? If you're not going to eat it, then don't waste it; those leftovers could feed three or four people." I'm now so aware that there are people who have so little.'

As part of their fundraising efforts before they went on their trip the group organised a fast whereby all the pupils in the school fasted for a day. They did the same again in the run up to Christmas 2003 in order to send more money to the Sisters of Mercy based in Mazabuka. 'They're always so glad of any help and we just wanted to give them a boost,' says David. 'They work long days 365 days of the year, so it's very tough on them; and they only get home to Ireland every two and a half years. Other than that they don't have any time off.'

'It was special for us doing the fast the second time because we knew exactly where the money was going,' says Christopher. 'We knew they'd already used a lot of the money we'd brought out with us to rebuild houses after the rainy season. There's always loads of rebuilding to be done after every rainy season: the houses are just made of mud and so when the rain comes the huts often fall down and the roofs cave in.'

When seven students from Sancta Maria College, Rathfarnham spent two weeks in the slums of Nairobi in June 2004 they were also immediately struck by the primitive housing. 'They weren't really houses at all,' says Emma Hassett. 'They were huts made from corrugated sheets. I remember we thought the first house we went into was awful, but then it turned out that it was beautiful in comparison to some others. The shacks were their houses and shops and everything; people had to pay rent for them and if they didn't pay up they were kicked out.

'They say you can drive around Nairobi all day and not see any slums because they're hidden away. We met a woman who lived only two streets away, but she'd never seen them; there's gates and security men at the end of her street so that the people from the slums can't get in. The government has no recognition of these slums at all. According to them, there are no slums; they don't appear on the maps of Nairobi and there's no account of the people living there. They're not registered; they don't have any birth certificates, and they simply don't exist to the government. There's no sewage system, so everything just runs down the middle of the street. We helped rake rubbish out of the sewers because if they get blocked the sewage spreads all over the street, so it's important to try and keep it flowing in the middle. The heat makes the smell from it really bad.

'The shacks were tiny and the people were living in them, sleeping in them and working in them,' says Helen Gaughan, one of three teachers who went on the trip. 'There was no water or electricity and a piece of wood might serve as the couch for a family of six. We went to one house where there was a sixteen-year-old girl looking after her younger siblings; their parents were dead and the baby had died from AIDS. She had been working full-time in a hairdressers and when she tried to start working part-time (so she could look after the kids) they fired her. I was quite upset;

I don't know if I was upset because some of the children were the same age or younger than my own two. It's just awful when I think of what my children have in comparison to those kids.'

The group visited four centres run by the Austrian-based charity, DKA, which had planned their itinerary. One of these was a place called Rescue Dada, an orphanage for girls who have been 'rescued' from the streets. 'They try and help the children catch up on their education, so they can go to school,' says Emma. 'They try and settle them down so they can be taught and so they do practical things, like woodwork and gardening, as well as schoolwork. They played soccer and basketball and we taught them how to do stretches.'

'We did some Irish dancing with the kids and they caught onto it so quickly,' says student Doireann Bregazzi-Neven. 'They did a rhythmic display of their dancing for us and they were amazing. Another time we saw a gymnastics display by some of the slum kids and you'd never see anything like it in the competitions here. They were making totem poles and pyramids out of five children!'

'Kids under seven are brought into Rescue Dada under court order and those over seven are encouraged to stay,' explains Helen. 'When they have been rehabilitated and they're ready to go to school DKA tries to find a family member or a foster family for the child. Primary education has been free in Kenya since 2003, but no new schools have been built and no new teachers appointed. The primary school population has increased from 5.7 to 7 million in recent years and because a lot of these children are orphans they need to board.

'We met an Irish Sister of Mercy nun, Sr Mary Killeen, who has founded four schools in Nairobi, and she says that in all her time working in Kenya she has come across only one girl from the streets aged over seven who hasn't been abused. That obviously means there's a huge risk of HIV spreading to children; and you know the myth about young girls. At one centre the children sang us songs about AIDS; the words went something like, "AIDS is killing our families" and I found that quite upsetting.

'Most of the children we met at Rescue Dada had been orphaned as a result of AIDS,' adds Doireann. 'We discovered some of the kids actually had parents still alive, but that they were drug addicts. We visited one centre, VIP, where we worked with kids our own age, but we didn't realise they were the same age as us because they looked like ten-year-olds. They sniff glue and petrol, which causes their brains to stop growing; and they're only expected to live to the age of twenty-five.

'We had brought loads of art materials with us: paper, paint and markers, and we did some art with them, but some of them couldn't really do it. They were hiding bottles of glue under their T-shirts and rags soaked in petrol and we had to keep leaving the room because we were getting dizzy, the smell of petrol and glue was that strong. My purse was taken by a boy who didn't come to the centre very often and when the other kids realised what had happened they were really upset and they said to me, "We will find that guy and we will punch him." They went and found him and one guy fractured his leg in the process of chasing him; they found the purse and most of the money and gave it back to me.'

'The idea in the centre is to distract the kids from sniffing glue and petrol and to keep them for as long as they can until they can refer them to another centre,' says Emma. 'It's like a halfway house, other places won't take the kids until they've stopped sniffing. It was awful to see them – all the skin under their noses was burnt.'

'There were guys working in the centre who were rehabilitated to a large extent and some of the artists were brilliant,' says Helen. 'Although they were recovered, they were still living in the slums. You could see it gave the children great dignity that the Sancta Maria pupils spent time with them; they were all so delighted. I remember we also met a girl in the slums who is on the Kenyan women's football team.'

The Dublin students played a soccer match at another centre called MUSA, which aims to prevent idleness and crime in the slums. 'They do sport, music and drama there,' says Emma. 'These guys were directly from the slums and some of them were amazing at football, even though they didn't have shoes and they were playing in bare feet on gravel. All the activities they do at the centre are all about developing their talents. Some of the staff are from the slums, too, and they act as role models for the kids. It didn't take long at all before the children became affectionate with us; they came over and stroked our skin and our hair because they were amazed by it. We heard little bits about their lives, but we didn't ask too many questions. When we were there we just had to keep going because there was so much going on, you didn't have time to think and it was only when I came back to Ireland that it started to hit me how sad their lives are.'

The pupils from John Scottus, St Joseph's and Sancta Maria all had to spend months working hard at fundraising before they made their trips overseas. Plant sales, coffee mornings, no uniform days, bag packing, church collections and individual donations all helped contribute to funds. The €30,000 plus the Sancta Maria pupils raised will go towards the building of a drug rehabilitation clinic. 'DKA is hoping that the Kenyan government will give them land for the centre; if they do, what we've raised will be used to build a centre,' says Helen. 'If they don't, it will be used to buy land, although I think DKA and Sr Mary are fairly hopeful the government will give them the land they need.'

During the trip Emma found herself at times 'worrying' about whether or not they were making any difference to the kids' lives. Nevertheless, she would love to make a return visit. 'It was a good experience and I'd definitely go again,' she says. 'I would go back next week, if I could. People ask me why I want to go back and I still don't have a good answer for them.

'I suppose I'd just love to do more.'

Jim and
Molly Buckley

who would choose
voluntary work over
television viewing any day

There is no doubt that Jim and Molly Buckley from Tullamore, Co. Offaly make a truly mighty volunteering partnership. Between them, they devote huge amounts of energy and resources to elderly and homeless people, people with disabilities, Travellers, victims of domestic violence and the GAA. Rather than spending endless hours plonked in front of the television, they prefer to spend their evenings and weekends helping people less fortunate than themselves.

Molly first became involved in voluntary work soon after she returned to work as a public health nurse in 1988, having spent the previous ten years as a full-time mum to the couple's five children. She has never forgotten one of the first routine house calls she made after her return to work. 'I found this woman living in a dark room at the back of her daughter's house,' she remembers. 'She was in a wheelchair and she never, ever went anywhere. She was stuck there seven days a week with no opportunity to do anything other than lie in bed or, occasionally, sit in a chair. It was a terrible situation.'

Molly immediately made enquiries to find out about the nearest branch of the Irish Wheelchair Association, only to discover that the local branch had been inactive for some time. She called a meeting, by the end of which she was elected the new chairperson; and so she became instrumental in the revival of the branch. One of the first steps taken by the committee was the acquisition of a wheelchair-accessible bus, which has made a huge difference to people's lives. 'Every weekend the bus brings people to Mass, which is very important,' says Molly. 'It also brings them on whatever outings they want to make and in the summer we organise picnics and go up the mountains.'

Given her commitment and enthusiasm, it was only a matter of time before Molly was elected regional representative of the Irish Wheelchair Association, then chairperson of the regional committee, and subsequently to the national executive. For six years she was vice-chairperson and then in 2002 she was elected chairperson, making her the first woman to hold the position. It is perhaps not a particularly surprising track record when one considers Molly's strong stance on certain issues. 'I have always been very strong on human and civil rights,' she says. 'And I see disability as a human and civil rights issue.'

Her strongly held belief that everyone should be treated with equal respect led to her involvement with Travellers and, since her election to Tullamore Urban Council in 1992 and to Offaly County Council in 1999, she has taken the opportunity again and again to speak on behalf of Travellers. She says, 'I support Travellers being treated as equal and being allowed to continue their own culture; and a lot of them come to me about housing and accommodation and issues that concern them.

'There has been an official halting site in Tullamore since 1986 – there are sixteen bays and the site has been done up recently and it's looking absolutely beautiful. Two unofficial sites have grown up around it, however, and we're now trying to put in more facilities so we can phase out the unofficial sites and ensure that people get appropriate accommodation. The local residents have been very angry that the unofficial sites have been allowed to develop and the Travellers themselves don't like it either because they don't want to live like that. Some would like to live on an official site and some on a transient site where they can come and go, while others would like standard housing. So there's a whole variety of accommodation needs.'

Molly has been on the council's traveller accommodation committee for five years now, with Travellers being represented by two members of the Tullamore Travellers Movement; and Molly has enjoyed getting to know Travellers personally. 'I have a very good relationship with all the Travellers here; and they with me,' she says. 'I've got to know a lot about their culture and way of life. I love to go down to the site in the evening and just sit chatting with them in their caravans. Often I'd be going back with an answer to something they'd asked me to find out and I enjoy spending time with them. Their caravans are just fabulous – you could eat your dinner off the floor, they're kept so lovely.'

Several years ago Molly was amazed by the response of staff from the Midlands Health Board when she presented a seminar on intercultural awareness with two of her Traveller friends. 'They were very angry when they heard how Travellers often have to live without water and that they may not get hospital appointments that they should be getting,' she says. 'In fact, when they heard the facts they were almost ready to go out and march for Travellers' rights. Many of them had never spoken to a Traveller before and it just shows how important it is to take the time to understand. It's the same with people with disabilities: if people just took the time to get know somebody with a disability they'd realise that they're people first and foremost.'

Molly admits that the whole Traveller accommodation issue can be 'very emotive' and she frequently comes across opposition. 'Quite a number of people around town would totally disagree with my approach and with my attitude,' she says. 'Something I say regularly is that if this situation was happening in a Third World country we'd all be up in arms sending money, but because it's on our own doorstep we don't. There was one council meeting where I spoke about Travellers' rights and the fact that they're human beings and the next day a man stopped me on the street and said, "Well done! I don't agree with what you said, but well done anyway." So some people admire me for taking a stand, even if they don't agree with me. I'd say roughly half the comments I get are positive and half are negative; a lot of people say nothing and I have been shunned a number of times for the stance I take. But I just say to myself that I know what I believe is right and I am quite prepared to battle on.'

Bridget 'Pinkie' McInerney was one of the two Travellers who led the intercultural awareness seminar with Molly. It is something she does regularly with healthcare workers and she hopes soon to be conducting workshops with council workers, Gardaí and members of community groups that are involved with Travellers. 'We talk about Travellers' culture and needs, and the barriers that exist for Travellers within the health board; we also bring up barriers that are there for the health board dealing with Travellers,' says Bridget. 'We come across a lot of ignorance: the first thing we do is to ask them to describe what they think people in Irish society think of Travellers and it always comes up that Travellers are dirty and rowdy. We address that by pointing out that a Traveller's caravan is very small and so you can't hold everything inside a caravan; half the stuff has to be outside. By the end of a workshop there's always a change in people's perceptions of Travellers and over the last few years Travellers have noticed a change in attitude from health board staff, which we believe is as a result of the workshops.'

Along with six other Travellers in Co. Offaly, Bridget underwent four years of training to become a primary health care worker for Travellers with the Midlands Health Board, which involves liaising between Travellers and health board staff. She lives on the roadside at Clara and longs for the day she can move into a group housing scheme. 'I've been fifteen years on the housing list, looking for Traveller-specific accommodation,' she says. 'To be honest, in the summer months it's nice to be living in a caravan, but in the winter it is complete hardship. I've got eight children, so you can imagine what it's like trying to wash eight children at the side of the road when it's freezing cold and get them ready for school while it's still dark. It's complete torture. My hands are very bad with arthritis from using cold water all the time; I don't think I can face another winter at the side of the road.'

Bridget is full of admiration for Molly's tireless work on behalf of Travellers. 'She is very good and she speaks up very well in the council and always brings up Traveller issues. If it wasn't for Molly, things would be an awful lot worse. She had a big hand in the refurbishment of the halting site in Tullamore a couple of years ago and she has been involved in the setting up of a temporary site; she also helps Travellers who want to live in standard housing. It would be great if more people took the time to get to know Travellers, like Molly has. People would know then exactly what it's like for Travellers, just like she does.

'A lot of people actually have a fear of Travellers because they don't know Travellers and I do think there's a lack of communication both ways. You need to get to know and to meet people and talk to them to break down the barriers and we're hoping that's what it will be like in the future. There's still a lot of councils that don't consult with Travellers and if halting sites and group housing schemes are going to work then it's very important that councils listen to what Travellers want and let them be involved in where they want to live. It would be brilliant if more settled people were like Molly and I always make sure all Travellers vote for her in the elections because I don't know where we'd be without her.'

Molly is in no doubt that her strong stance on human rights issues has cost her votes – not so much in local elections, but certainly when she stood as an Independent Health Alliance candidate in the last general election. 'There's no doubt about it,' she says, 'I lost votes because I was standing mainly on rights issues – rights for people with disabilities and rights for Travellers – as well as on issues like housing and childcare. I got 1800 first preference votes and, by the time I was eliminated, I had 2800 votes. I wasn't happy with the result.

'I work day and night for people and certainly the amount of work I do was not reflected in the vote I got, but then they're not popular issues – they're issues that people see as important, but not as top priority. At the end of the day it was an election of greed – social inclusion and social issues didn't come into it at all. I was totally fed up for a few weeks, but then I've said all along that you don't do these things to get a return; and once I was over it I was flying again. There's no doubt about it, but I would like to be doing the same kind of things at national level – because that's where policy is made and an awful lot of local issues depend on national policy – but I don't know if I'll stand again. I don't think my family would want me to; Jim was very hurt about it because he knows how much work I do. And he does equally as much.'

Jim became involved with homeless people in 1988 when he attended a couple of public meetings that were called by the sisters of the Convent of Mercy because there were three young women sleeping rough on the convent doorstep. By the end of the second meeting he found himself elected onto a committee to address the issue of homelessness in the area. He was then nominated chairman – a position he didn't want to fill because of his workload as assistant principal officer in the Department of Social Welfare in Tullamore and his heavy involvement with the GAA, which meant he had little spare time. But, after giving the matter some thought, he changed his mind and, to this day, he is still chairman of the committee.

Before seeking suitable accommodation to house homeless people the committee decided to carry out a survey to ascertain the full extent of the problem. 'We contacted the Marian Hostel on High Street, the Convent of Mercy, the parochial house and the Garda station – any place where people out of home might go in search of help,' says Jim. 'We did that over a period of three months – not just looking at people sleeping rough long-term, but also at instances, say, where a young fellow comes home drunk and is kicked out for a week or when someone leaves home temporarily after a family row – that kind of thing.

'We then looked at what Focus Point were doing in Dublin and Vincent de Paul in Cavan and Carlow. We didn't find any suitable building in Tullamore and so we decided that we would have to build new purpose-built accommodation. We eventually bought Lann Elo in early 1990 and we received funding from the

Department of the Environment to build eight one-bedroom and two two-bedroom units and a manager's residence.

'The urban council kept playing down the extent of the problem because the definition of homeless at that time was very rigid – you had to be literally sleeping rough for at least six months before you were considered homeless. And yet it took us only an hour to fill the ten units! And if we had had another forty units we would have filled them too. Since then we have had single people, married couples and single mothers with their children and because there has been such a demand – as many as twenty-five people may apply to fill one unit – we are about to build a further thirteen units, including three emergency ones. We had hoped to have people in and out fairly fast, but most people have to wait a long time before they are housed by the council.'

What motivates Jim to continue his voluntary work? 'I suppose knowing there is a problem and being able to do something about it. If you help somebody, if you solve a problem – there is satisfaction in that. And I suppose that keeps you going. I've also been involved in the GAA for years, since my lads were old enough to play hurling. I started out training underage teams and was secretary to the senior football team and Irish Officer on the county board for six years. Somebody asked me recently if I watch much television and I told him I only watch a small bit of sport occasionally; I'm a lot happier out on the GAA pitch or even at a meeting.'

And what motivates Molly? 'I suppose knowing that there are so many people without a voice, people who have never heard of the Celtic Tiger,' she says. 'There is so much poverty and there are so many people forgotten about; I enjoy trying to change things a little bit. A lot of councillors don't give people much time, but I think it is so important to sit down with people and listen to them, giving them the dignity of knowing that they're important. That in itself means a lot. And then if the issue can be solved in some kind of way, it's a bonus really. I get great satisfaction out of helping people with their problems. Absolutely!'

As well as her work with Travellers and people with disabilities, Molly is also chairperson of The Rights for the

Elderly, which is in the course of building sixteen houses and a community centre in Tullamore. She has also started helping victims of domestic violence, which resulted from her involvement with the Emergency Shelter Committee. 'We prioritised women who had experienced domestic violence and we saw a great need for accommodation,' she says. 'There is a refuge, but there's only four family units and if somebody is in an emergency situation we sometimes have to get them into a B&B or into a refuge in another part of the country, so we really need to get some kind of emergency accommodation. We also have an information and counselling service and a helpline, which we work on a rota basis; every weekend in four I have to be around to respond to whatever comes up.'

Molly's tireless efforts were finally recognised in 1996 when she was voted Offaly Person of the Year. 'It was a great honour all together,' she says. 'I didn't expect it. It was amazing really; an unbelievable honour to get.' More recently, she received a well-deserved boost in the 2004 local elections when she was re-elected to both Offaly County Council and Tullamore Town Council. She headed the poll in the latter, becoming the first ever Independent and first ever woman to do so.

There can be little doubt that Molly and Jim will continue to devote much of their spare time for the good of others. 'There are a lot of smug people out there who are moving in their own circles and they just don't know what's going on outside their own little world,' says Jim. 'And yet some day one of these issues, like homelessness or drugs, could affect their own family. Drugs are so common in Tullamore now, like everywhere else. Our kids aren't perfect, but thank God they're all doing OK so far. But you certainly can't be smug. All you can do is hope.'

Mary Kennedy and Eva Foster

who found Africa
'got into their blood'
when they went on a
Self Help trek
to Eritrea

Television presenter Mary Kennedy grew up in a house where voluntary work was seen as par for the course of everyday life; her parents were 'up to their necks' in it. While her father was involved in organisations like the Credit Union, St Vincent de Paul and Muintir na Tíre, her mother spent endless hours cleaning the local church in Clondalkin, turning wedding dresses into vestments and being involved in the Irish Countrywomen's Association. 'Growing up, I just accepted their community work as part of life and I do think that's where I got it from,' says Mary. 'Although it's probably only as an adult that I've looked back and reflected and seen that it was important and informative.'

Following the example set by her parents, Mary has undertaken voluntary work for some years now. She is involved with The Carers' Association and has been their patron since 2003; she is also on the board of The Aoibhneas Foundation, which provides refuge for women and children who have experienced domestic violence. While maintaining a keen involvement in both these organisations, she has recently set her volunteering sights somewhat further afield. From her teenage years she harboured a 'secret ambition' to visit Africa, although it was only in October 2002 that she finally realised her dream. The trip came about when the director of Self Help, Seamus Hayes, invited Mary to lead a trek in Eritrea. The organisation, which was set up by the Irish Farmers' Association in response to the Ethiopian famine in 1984, has projects in five countries: Ethiopia, Malawi, Uganda, Kenya and Eritrea; and Mary was asked to lead the fifth trek. While she was 'delighted' to be asked, she felt somewhat apprehensive. The fact that she was the first woman to be asked to lead the annual trek did not help; she was to follow in the footsteps of Mícheál Ó Muircheartaigh, John Creedon, Joe O'Brien and Ronan Collins. However, once she knew she could take the necessary time off work she did not think twice before answering in the affirmative. 'I love adventure and I love challenges,' she says.

Every year about fifty people from all over Ireland join the trek, with each participant having to raise a substantial sum of money; in 2002 the amount was €4,500. As leader, Mary was not obliged to fundraise, but she decided to raise the money, anyway, by running the Women's Mini Marathon, organising World Cup lunches and selling friends and neighbours' donations at car boot sales. She also asked her friend Eleanor Shanley, former member of De Danann, to do a concert in aid of Self Help. Having raised the necessary amount, Mary then invited her eldest daughter to join her on the trek. Eva, who had been unable to help much with fundraising because she was studying for her Leaving Certificate at the time, jumped at the opportunity.

'I think it's great that Eva experienced Africa at the age of eighteen because it broadens your horizons,' says Mary. 'Neither of us would have known what it's like if we hadn't gone there. You hear about people starving, but there's so much more to Africa than that. We saw that people in Eritrea want to develop, that they have the same aspirations, the same ideals and the same values we do. They've got great hope and great confidence and they're very hard workers; they're determined to improve their lives. They're only ten years independent from Ethiopia and so they are in the situation we were in eighty years ago, just starting off, and they deserve every bit of help they can get.'

What were Eva's first impressions of Eritrea? 'The airport was really tiny,' she recalls. 'It was like a landing strip in a field and there were lots of people just standing there, looking, seeing if they could get a glimpse of us. Everyone knew who we were; and everything we did while we were on the trek was reported in the newspapers.'

'It was like stepping back in time,' adds Mary, 'Especially when we went to the hotel, which was very basic. If it had had a little bit of money thrown at it, it could have been described as art deco! Walking from the hotel to the main boulevard in Asmara you were walking over broken roads; and yet there was a lovely atmosphere and Italian flavour to the city because it was colonised by Italy for many years. Travelling around the country, it was very moving to see abandoned jeeps and armoured cars, all left over from the war, and guns just thrown into ditches.'

Some days were spent trekking in the hills, others visiting various Self Help projects; and it didn't take the group long to realise the impact the organisation makes on people's lives. They were particularly struck by an irrigation system they saw in action. 'It was incredible the difference it made,' says Mary. 'You'd see sprinklers in a field of healthy corn and half a mile down the road, where there's no irrigation, you'd be looking at a field of dead corn. Usually Eritrea has rain twice a year, but when we visited there hadn't been any rain for eighteen months. One day, when we were driving along, our driver said you could see the drought kicking in because the animals were scrawny – you could see their bones sticking out through their skin. We didn't see any people starving to death, but we did see emaciated animals and we saw a dreadful kind of 'death' in the fields because it was so arid. Up around Keren people were dependent on aid and we saw them diving on the trucks when they arrived with food.'

Eva was particularly struck by a dried up river that they came across. 'We walked along the river bed and we were just walking on sand because it was totally dry,' she says. 'But we could see the river should have been really big and wide, like the Shannon. We also saw a well that was incredible; it was fifty metres deep and the men had to dig it themselves with shovels and spades. It took them three months.'

'That's the way of Self Help,' explains Mary. 'They want people to have a sense of being involved by doing the work themselves; and I think that's very important. Once the hole was dug, Self Help came and put in the pump and now the well services three villages. It was dug by five farmers who used to work for a landlord and the well means they can now grow their own produce, bring it to market and eventually pay back the loan; the money will then go on a project somewhere else. We also visited a women's enterprise where they were making honey and we saw some very impressive poultry programmes.'

Self Help operates by providing loans for the necessary materials to set up projects, but how big a difference do these loans actually make to people's lives? 'A huge, huge difference,' says Mary. 'You've no idea; it's impossible to contemplate. You go to visit a farmer and he's so proud; he brings you into his house, which is what we would call a shed made with concrete blocks, and beside it is the mud hut, which he used to live in until he took a loan from Self Help. He now uses it for storage and he keeps a pot-belly stove and cooks there.'

This contrasted sharply with the 'housing' Mary and Eva saw in towns like Massawa. 'There was one place where there were no floorboards or anything and you could see the bullets,' says Eva. 'The walls were cracked from bullet holes and yet there were people living inside.'

'Massawa was very, very poor,' agrees Mary. 'It was like a shanty town – people were living in cardboard and it was awful. In the back streets they put their beds, which were basically pallets, up against the wall during the day. The place was teeming with people and it was filthy. You didn't see people emaciated, but you did see a lot of filth, which makes it very difficult for them. We saw children on a scrap heap, playing with sticks and tyres, and the thing that fascinated me most was that the women wore these snow white shawls. I don't know how they kept them clean because after only a day our white T-shirts were destroyed by the clay and the dust.'

Mary was struck by how little it took to brighten up the lives of the Eritreans she met: children were thrilled to receive the lollipops, pencils and copy books that she'd bought before she left Ireland. A friend had given her one hundred dollars and asked her to make sure it was spent on children. 'We met people when we were going on our walks and we used to give them money,' says Mary. 'I can remember I met a Franciscan priest in a military graveyard; he was wearing frayed brown robes and we got chatting. It turned out he was the chaplain of the local school and so I decided to give the one hundred dollars to him because I trusted him. He was just so thrilled – it would probably have kept the school going for two years. I didn't think any more about it and later that day, while we were walking around the town, he came up to us in this clapped out jeep; he'd been driving around till he found me because he wanted to give me a relic of Padre Pio and a little prayer to St Anthony to say thank you. It was really, really nice of him; I think those kinds of things are special. He still writes to me and sends photos.'

The Self Help trekkers received a tremendous welcome wherever they visited in Eritrea, in both the Christian north and the Muslim south. 'We visited the Christian part of the country first and it was incredible because it was very matriarchal,' remembers Mary. 'You could see the power was very much with the women, they were running the credit unions and poultry programmes and they were the ones working in the fields. They had huge initiative and you didn't see the men at all. But it was the direct opposite when we went to the Muslim part of the country. Whereas in the Christian areas the women had welcomed us by throwing popcorn at us from their lovely handcrafted bowls and by singing a welcome warble, in the Muslim part it was the men who welcomed us with athletic displays of dancing over swords. They'd been told that the leader of the trek was a woman, but they still presented me with a two-hundred-year-old ceremonial sword and a traditional outfit for a man. It was incredible! The women, meanwhile, stood at the side and they wore stunningly beautiful saris in lime green, shocking pink and canary yellow. Absolutely gorgeous! When I went over to say hello to them they were just so warm and so welcoming; they were very comfortable in their role, it was what they were used to.'

'There was one place we went to and we were about two or three hours late,' remembers Eva. 'It was in the evening and we'd been out all day; the kids had been lining the streets for hours waiting for us. There was another place, where we weren't meant to stop, but everyone in the village was out waiting and they had made pancakes for us. And so we stopped.'

Mary remembers one village they visited where a thousand school children had spent hours waiting in the baking heat. 'They formed a guard of honour along the streets,' she says. 'They were just thrilled to see us and they had made lovely posters, which said, "We wish everlasting friendship between our countries". The welcome they gave us was like the welcome President McAleese received when she visited the local primary school there recently. It was huge. We had a cultural evening with the Eritreans, which was really nice, and we saw that, even though it was the other side of the world, the concerns of people are the same, no matter what: they had working songs, love songs, fighting songs and dances. And then we had a bit of a céilídh; we taught them some céilídh dances and it was great craic. I think those things are terribly important as part of a cultural interchange.'

'They say Africa gets into your blood,' says Mary, and for her daughter and herself this certainly seems to be true. As soon as they returned from Eritrea, Eva cast around her friends, looking for someone to join her on the following year's Self Help trek. 'I knew I wanted to go back to Africa as soon as I got home,' she says. 'I just had to find somebody to go with me and so I asked my friend, Triona Hefferon.'

The 2003 Self Help trek was to take place in Uganda and Eleanor Shanley was asked to lead the trek, her interest in the organisation having resulted from the fundraising concert she had done the previous year. And so Eva spent months fundraising; she joined her mum running the Women's Mini Marathon, she had a car boot sale and she returned to her former school of Loreto High School, Beaufort and asked the pupils to hold a no-uniform day (they did and they raised €600). Also, Liam Lawton helped her out by holding a concert in the National Concert Hall.

How did Eva find the Ugandan experience in comparison to Eritrea? 'It was very different because Uganda is a lot greener,' she says. 'There was lots of rain while we were there and we nearly got drowned one day on the side of a mountain. There were loads of banana trees and that's what people lived on; that's all they ate from one day to the next. We did some treks, but we couldn't get to see any of the projects because of the political unrest; it just wasn't safe for us to travel outside of the towns. I was disappointed because it's nice to see what Self Help does and how people live. One day, however, all of the farmers and the other people involved in the projects came to visit us in the town where we were staying and they talked to us about what Self Help had done for them. They put on a play about how Self Help had changed their lives and they brought a huge board with pictures of the different projects. It's a very volatile part of the world, however, and I've since heard that one of the projects has been suspended because of landmines in the area, and the farmers are living in refugee camps.'

The trek in October 2004 will take place in Ethiopia; Mary and Eva have both signed up and they have been busy fundraising €4,750 each. This time the trek will be led by Tracy Piggott and Mary is looking forward to being able to stand with folded arms and say, 'Well done, Tracy. That was a lovely speech'! Neither Mary nor Eva knows exactly how Ethiopia will compare to their previous African experiences, although they have been warned by Self Helpers who have visited the country before that they will see people lying on the ground 'totally emaciated'. Mary says, 'When we were in Eritrea, Ethiopians were seen as the oppressors and it will be interesting to see how the Ethiopians view their neighbours. Perhaps they will say, "Aren't the Eritreans very selfish? They have two ports and they won't let us have one of them." That's the swings and roundabouts of there being two sides to every story.'

Mary is in no doubt that visiting Africa is a life-changing experience. 'Our traditional view of people in Africa is that they're totally struggling and that they'll never really get out from under the yoke, but to meet Africans and get to know them you realise that they have the same values, aspirations, goals and energies as we have. And the same rights. They just need a bit of a dig out. Certainly in Eritrea I was struck by their energy, although maybe in Ethiopia it will be different.'

So why are Mary and Eva so keen to continue their involvement with Self Help? 'I suppose it's nice to help other people, like the people in Africa who aren't as well off as we are,' says Eva. 'It's not a huge thing to raise a few bob for them because even a small amount goes so far in Africa: they can do so much with it, like the one hundred dollars for the school would have gone a long way, much further than it would here. It's just nice to help people out and it's nice to go and visit another country. I've also made a lot of friends on the treks and I still keep in contact with them. We're always talking on the phone and I've gone and visited them and they've come and stayed here. We also meet up from time to time at various fundraisers: when Liam Lawton performed in the National Concert Hall people came from as far away as Monaghan, Clare, Louth, Wicklow and the midlands.'

And Mary? 'I definitely do have this total conviction that we must have a commitment to looking out for people who are less well off than ourselves, in our own environment, but also abroad. You hear some people say, "Well, there's plenty to spend your money on here; charity begins at home". But if everybody had that attitude it would be a terrible loss because a tiny amount of money raised here can make a huge difference to a whole community in Africa. I feel we have enough money and energy to shell it out there as well as here; there's no reason why we shouldn't do both. I definitely think people should be more aware of what's happening overseas.'

'I feel that's what I want to do, to give some time and energy to charity at home and abroad. I think there's no reason why everyone can't do that. Everybody has their skills, I can't do committees because of my work schedule, but if somebody asks me to do MC for a fundraising event I'm happy to do it. I give a bit of time to The Carers' Association: I raise awareness in any way I can and, as their patron, I host their balls, I give interviews and I do voiceovers for their radio ads. I do similar kind of work for Aoibhneas, but I do feel that somebody in my position gets off very lightly because I come in at the end when the work is done. And then I give energy to Self Help and, more recently, to GOAL. I was asked to visit GOAL's homes for street children in Calcutta in August this year in order to raise awareness. I had been to Calcutta once before for Mother Teresa's funeral and I was thrilled to make a return trip. GOAL has a similar philosophy to Self Help, about involving local people, and the homes are run by two local paediatricians who have been with the organisation for twenty-seven years and who have brought in other local people. I have to admit, though, that I wasn't prepared for the scale of the poverty and squalor. It was my first visit to the slums and the red-light districts and my heart went out to the "poorest of the poor", as Mother Teresa referred to the homeless and destitute of Calcutta. It was impossible not to be moved by the sight of children begging or scavenging in the dumps and you couldn't walk any distance without stepping over people sleeping on the streets. The noise was deafening and the stench was nauseating, but the people were wonderful: they were gentle, dignified and grateful for the help provided by aid agencies like GOAL. There's no doubt in my mind that these people deserve everything we can do for them. I've said it before and I say it again: where we live on this earth is an accident of birth and those of us in the more affluent parts of the world have a moral responsibility to look to the needs of those who are struggling.'

Mary reckons there would be 'something missing' from her life if she was not involved in charitable work. 'I think everyone has a moral obligation to do something – not just those of us who are in the public eye,' she says. 'Being in the public eye means you can bring something different to it, but everybody has their skills, some people are great fundraisers, some great organisers and others great ralliers. I hate asking people for money; I ran the Dublin City Marathon twice without raising money (I was too shy to ask people to sponsor me), although more recently I ran a half marathon on the Aran Islands in aid of the medical research centre in Crumlin Hospital and I've run the mini marathon three times in aid of Self Help. I'm useless at asking people for money: the first time I went around doors looking for sponsorship I stood back while my friend knocked on the doors! I do find fundraising is hard work, but it's also very sociable and there's a lovely sense of community when people get involved in it. We have had to raise the guts of ten grand between the two of us to go to Ethiopia, but you can multiply that by five for the effect that will have there. It will make a huge difference.

'I feel everybody has the responsibility to get involved in some kind of voluntary work. At the end of the day it's not just about 'doing good'. You also get a huge amount out of it; first of all, an appreciation of how bloody well off we are in Ireland, and also a great sense of community. We have great fun and there's this kind of community spirit, which is really, really special. Like Eva said, you make great friends and I think that's true once you become involved in any organisation. I advise people, if they're feeling lonely, to go and join something – *do* some voluntary work. Not only will you be helping other people, but you'll also get a huge amount out of it yourself.'

Appendix

Volunteering Ireland
Coleraine House
Coleraine Street
Dublin 7
01 8722622
www.volunteeringireland.com

Voluntary Service International
30 Mountjoy Square
Dublin 1
01 8551011
vsi@iol.ie

Slí Eile Volunteer Communities
20 Upper Gardiner Street
Dublin 1
01 8787167
www.jesuit.ie

i-to-i Ireland
Exploration House
26 Main Street
Dungarvan
Co. Waterford
058 40050
www.i-to-i.com

Irish Hospice Foundation
Morrison Chambers
32 Nassau Street
Dublin 2
01 6793188
www.hospice-foundation.ie

Oxfam Ireland
9 Burgh Quay
Dublin 2
01 6727662
www.oxfam.ie

Amnesty International Irish Section
48 Fleet Street
Dublin 2
01 6776361
www.amnesty.ie

Chernobyl Children's Project
Ballycurreen Industrial Estate
Kinsale Road
Cork
021 4312999
www.chernobyl-ireland.com

The Lost Riders Motorcycle Club
9 Westbrook Drive
Balbriggan
Co. Dublin
01 8417014 or 087 2485943

The Joey Dunlop Foundation
4 Windermere Ave
Lakeside Gardens
Onchan
Isle of Man IM3 2DT
0044 1624 628089

WAVE Trauma Centre
5 Chichester Park South
Belfast BT15 5DW
Northern Ireland
028 90779922
www.wavetc.clara.net

Billy Riordan Memorial Trust
Kilfountain Road
Dingle
Co. Kerry
087 2835615
00 265 924195
www.billysmalawiproject.com

Cultural Links
1 Rathcormack
Fermoy
Co. Cork
025 37940

Community Mothers Programme
Park House
North Circular Road
Dublin 7
01 8387122

Bodywhys
PO Box 105
Blackrock
Co. Dublin
01 2834963
www.bodywhys.ie

GOAL
PO Box 19
Dun Laoghaire
Co. Dublin
01 2809779
www.goal.ie

Irish Society for the Prevention of
Cruelty to Animals
Derryglogher Lodge
Keenagh
Co. Longford
043 25035
www.ispca.ie

Sight Savers International
2 Bayview Drive
Killiney
Co. Dublin
01 2353996
www.sightsavers.org

The Irish Cancer Society
5 Northumberland Road
Dublin 4
01 2310500
www.cancer.ie

The Jack and Jill Children's
Foundation
Johnstown Manor
Johnstown
Naas
Co. Kildare
045 894538
www.jackandjill.ie

Folamh
251-255 Richmond Road
Fairview
Dublin 3
01 8843214
www.smartbusiness.ie

Simon Community of Ireland
St Andrew's House
28-30 Exchequer Street
Dublin 2
01 6711606
www.simoncommunity.ie

Society of St Vincent de Paul
8 New Cabra Road
Dublin 7
01 8384164
www.svp.ie

Corrymeela
5 Drumaroan Road
Ballycastle
Co. Antrim BT54 6QU
Northern Ireland
028 20762626
www.corrymeela.org

Comhlámh
10 Upper Camden Street
Dublin 2
01 4783490
www.comhlamh.org

Irish Wheelchair Association
Áras Chuchulainn
Blackheath Drive
Clontarf
Dublin 3
01 8186455
www.iwa.ie

Disability Federation of Ireland
Fumbally Court
Fumbally Lane
Dublin 8
01 4547978
www.disability-federation.ie

Irish Travellers' Movement
4-5 Eustace Street
Dublin 2
01 6796577
www.itmtrav.com

Church Missionary Society
Overseas House
3 Belgrave Road
Rathmines
Dublin 6
01 4970931
www.cmsireland.org

Dublin Gospel Choir
PO Box 702
Maynooth
Co. Kildare
01 6270298
www.dublingospelchoir.com

Operation Christmas Child
Gledswood Lodge
Bird Avenue
Clonskeagh
Dublin 14
01 2695055
www.samaritanspurse.ie

The Carers Association
Prior's Orchard
John's Quay
Co. Kilkenny
1800 240724
www.carersireland.com

The Aoibhneas Foundation
PO Box 5504
Coolock
Dublin 17
01 8670805
www.aoibhneas.org

Self Help
Hacketstown
Co. Carlow
059 6471175
www.selfhelp.ie